Common Dividend

A STUDY OF MODERN MONEY, DEBT SLAVERY AND DESTRUCTIVE ECONOMICS

BY
RUDOLF RICKES

USA ▪ Canada ▪ UK ▪ Ireland

Note for Librarians: A cataloguing record for this book is available from Library and Archives Canada at www.collectionscanada.ca/amicus/index-e.html
ISBN 1-4251-0784-2

PUBLISHING™

Offices in Canada, USA, Ireland and UK

Book sales for North America and international:
Trafford Publishing, 6E–2333 Government St.,
Victoria, BC V8T 4P4 CANADA
phone 250 383 6864 (toll-free 1 888 232 4444)
fax 250 383 6804; email to orders@trafford.com
Book sales in Europe:
Trafford Publishing (UK) Limited, 9 Park End Street, 2nd Floor
Oxford, UK OX1 1HH UNITED KINGDOM
phone 44 (0)1865 722 113 (local rate 0845 230 9601)
facsimile 44 (0)1865 722 868; info.uk@trafford.com
Order online at:
trafford.com/06-2542

10 9 8 7 6 5 4 3

DEDICATED TO THE POOR

PRESENTATION

The sound and effective financial system, which we will discuss in this small volume, is the financial system generally known under the name of "Social Credit", not applied yet anywhere, but of which the principles were established by the Scottish Engineer and Economist C. H. Douglas, propagated since through a whole school in a great many countries.

"The gentle reader will notice, that occasionally an other name will appear in this pamphlet namely "Common Dividend". This name was only selected because it is "Synonymous" with "Social Credit" and it was chosen to prevent an infringement with the name Social Credit of a party in B. C. in case of a publication. Otherwise, there is no deviation from the principles of the founder. H. Douglas and the Pilgrims of the "Social Credit Movement." Furthermore I have to acknowledge, that I have copied, – as mentioned on the front page of this pamphlet already with the title "Common Dividend", – the entire contents of it from literature obtainable to me and is therefore a 100% spiritual property of the "Pilgrims of the Social Credit Movement, always signed with the Authors name when given, of course. Rudolf Rickes."

Douglas expressed propositions, which, once put into practice, would conclusively eliminate all financial problems where there is no physical problem of production or distribution. His system gives finance a role of service, and no more one of command, in the country's economy.

Douglas drew up his propositions with precision, but without entering into the methods of their implementation. Besides, he pointed out that these methods can be various, according to the different places, established customs, etc., and modifiable according to the results from experience, but without straying from the principles.

We think that our role is, above all, to show what men must get from their economic activities. Also, the why, the reasons why they are entitled to these results.

As for the how, how to put Douglas's propositions into application to achieve these results, in our opinion, it is rather a matter for experts. Experts, not ministers nor governments; the role of the latter being rather to dictate what to do to the experts, letting them decide the how.

It is with this knowledge in mind that Douglas, addressing one day a meeting of Social Creditors, said that, according to him, it is the bankers who will establish the Social Credit financial system—of course when they will receive the order to do so.

On an other occasion, he suggested that, in order to get out of the financial rut into which individuals and governments are groaning during the last decades, the government ought to assemble a few of the country's leading bankers, lock them up and keep them locked up, until they find a remedy to the evils, which afflicts the world. (This remedy, they will have found it quickly!)

However, in the present work, we are getting a little into the how. How one could implement Douglas's propositions. How to establish a constant equilibrium between prices and the purchasing power in the public's hand. How one could finance any new production, not with savings, but with new credits.

Our goal is simply to show the possibility of the implementation of Douglas's propositions, not to present this way as the only possible one. The methods set out here are, therefore, neither dogmatic nor exclusive. But we advocate what seems to us to be more practical, less disconcerting, generously making use of the existing financial mechanisms, while purging them radically of the fundamental financial defect which diverts them from the real end of the economy: the service of human needs.

"Michael", the Social Credit Journal and other writings from the same source, have refrained generally from entering into the domain of the possible methods of establishing a financial system in keeping with Douglas's principles.

CONTENTS

Presentation 5

1. The Money Myth Exposed Common Dividend Part I 9

2. Why We Demand "Common Dividend" 23

3. A Dividend For Everyone 25

4. A Debt Money System 26

5. To Correct What Is Wicked 29

6. A Super Power Dominates Governments 30

7. The Blood Of Economic Life 32

8. A Constitutional Monetary Power 34

9. Abraham Lincoln And John F. Kennedy 36

10. The Federal Reserve Act 39

11. A Lesson To Learn 41

12. Quotes On Money 42

13. Thoughts About Unemployment Or War 44

14. The Nature Of Credit, Sacred And Profane 45

15. What Do We Mean By "Real Common Dividend" 46

16. Various Excerpts From The Social Creditor 53

17. A "Party", The Opposite Of Social Credit 54

18. For A Powerful People 56

19. Present Taxes Are A Robbery 57

20. 80% Of Your Income Tax Pays The Interest On National Debt 60

21. Guernsey's Monetary Experiment 61

22. The Young People Want A New Financial System 65

23. Social Credit, For A Healthy Economy—the Michael Journal 68

24. Toward Social Credit By Apostolate And Tenacity 80

25. Conclusion 83

26. Supplement: The Monetary System During The "Third Reich" 84

27. Common Dividend Part II 85

28. Common Dividend Part III 101

29. The Greatest Swindle Of All Times 106

30. Appendix 114

31. World Government 121

COMMON DIVIDEND
PART I

THE MONEY MYTH EXPOSED

LOUIS EVEN

Shipwreck survivors

An explosion had blown their ship apart. Each one grasped the first bit of wreckage that came to hand. And when it was over there were five left, five huddled on a raft, which the waves carried along at their will. As for the other victims of the disaster, there was no sign of them.

Hour after long hour their eyes searched the horizon. Would some passing ship sight them? Would their makeshift raft find its way to some friendly shore?

Suddenly a cry rang out: "Look ! Look! Over there, in the direction the waves are carrying us!"

And as the vague silhouette proved itself to be, in fact, the outline of a shore, the figures on the raft danced with joy.

They were five, five Canadians. There was Frank, the carpenter, big and energetic. It was he who had first cried, "Land!"

Then Paul, a farmer, next is Jim, an animal breeder, and then there is Harry, an agriculturist and finally Tom, a prospector and mineralogist.

A Providential island

To our five men, setting foot on land was like returning from life to the grave. When they had dried and warmed themselves, their first impulse was to explore this little island on to which they had been cast, far from civilization.

A quick survey was sufficient to raise their spirit. The island was not a barren rock. True enough, they were the only men on it at the moment. But judging from the herds of semi-domesticated animals they encountered, there must have been men here at some time before them. Jim, the animal breeder, was sure he could completely domesticate them and put them to good service.

Paul found the island's soil, for the most part, to be quite suitable for cultivation.

Harry discovered some fruit trees, which, if properly tended, would give good harvest. Most important were the large stands of timber embracing many types of wood. Frank, without too much difficulty, would be able to build houses for the little community.

As for Tom, the prospector, well, the rock formations of the island showed signs of rich mineral deposits. Lacking the tools, Tom still felt his ingenuity and initiative could produce metals from the ores.

So each could serve the common good with his special talent. All agreed to call the place Salvation Island. All gave thanks to Providence for the reasonably happy ending to what could have been a terrible tragedy.

True wealth

The men are at work. The carpenter builds houses and makes furniture. At first they find their food where they can. But soon the fields are tilled and seeded, and the farmer has his crops.

As season followed season this island, this heritage of the five men, Salvation Island, became richer and richer.

Its wealth was not that of gold or of paper bank notes, but one of true value; a wealth of food and clothing and shelter, of all the things to meet human needs.

Each man worked at his own trade. Whatever surpluses he might have of his own produce, he exchanged for the surplus products of others.

Life wasn't always as smooth and complete as they could have wished it to be. They lacked many of the things to which they had been accustomed in civilization. But their lot could have been a great deal worse.

Besides, all had experienced the depression in Canada. They still remembered the empty bellies side by side with stores crammed with food.

At least, on Salvation Island, they weren't forced to see the things they needed rot before their eyes. Taxes were unknown here. Nor did they go in constant fear of seizure by the bailiff. They worked hard but at least they could enjoy the fruits of their toil.

So they developed the island, thanking God and hoping for the day of reunion with their families, still in possession of life and health, those two greatest of blessings.

A serious inconvenience

Our men often got together to talk over their affairs.

Under the simple economic system, which had developed, one thing was beginning to bother them more and more; they had no form of money. Barter, the direct exchange of goods for goods, had its drawbacks. The products to be exchanged were not always at hand when a trade was discussed. For example, wood delivered to the farmer in winter could not be paid for in potatoes until six months later.

Sometimes one man might have an article of considerable size, which he wished to exchange for a number of smaller articles produced by different men at different times.

All this complicated business and laid a heavy burden on the memory. With a monetary system, however, each one could sell his products to the others for money.

With this money he could buy from the others the things he wanted, when he wished and when they were available.

It was agreed that a system of money would indeed be very convenient. But none of them knew how to set up such a system. They knew how to produce true wealth – goods. But how to produce money, the symbol of this wealth, was something quite beyond them. They were ignorant of the origin of money, and needing it didn't know how to produce it. Certainly, many men of education would have been in the same boat; all our governments were in that predicament during the ten years prior to the war. The only thing the country lacked at that time was money, and the governments apparently didn't know what to do to get it.

Arrival of a refugee

One evening when our boys were sitting on the beach going over their problem for the hundreds time, they suddenly saw approaching a small boat with a solitary man on the oars.

They learned that he was a refugee from war-torn, central Europe. Along with other emigrants he had boarded a ship bound for Australia.

A storm had driven their ship on to a reef. He was the only survivor of the wreck. His name Oliver Glücksterlingmann. They could remember only his first name.

Delighted to have a new companion, they provided him with the best they had and took him on an inspection tour of the colony.

"Even though we're lost and cut off from the rest of the world," they told him, "we haven't too much to complain about. The earth and the forest are good to us. We lack only one thing – money. That would make it easier for us to exchange our products."

"Well, you can thank Providence," replied Oliver" because I am a banker and in no time at all I'll set up a system of money guaranteed to satisfy you. Then you'll have everything that people in civilization have."

A banker !....A BANKER !... An angel coming down out of the clouds couldn't have inspired more reverence and respect in our men. For, after all, are we not accustomed, we people in civilization, to genuflect before bankers, those men who control the lifeblood of finance?

Civilization's God

"Mr. Oliver, as our banker, your only occupation on this island will be to look after our money; no manual labor."

"I shall, like every other banker, carry out to complete satisfaction my task of forging the community's prosperity."

"Mr. Oliver, we're going to build you a house, that will be in keeping with your dignity as a banker. But in the meantime, do you mind if we lodge you in the building we use for our get together?"

That will suit me, my friends. But first at all, unload my boat. There's paper, and a printing press complete with ink and type; and there's a little barrel which I exhort you to treat with the greatest care."

They unloaded everything. The small barrel aroused intense curiosity in our good fellows.

"This barrel," Oliver announced, "contains treasure beyond dreams. It if full of ...gold!"

Full of gold! the five all but swooned. The god of civilization here on Salvation Island! The yellow God, always hidden, yet terrible in its power; whose presence or absence or slightest caprice could decide the very fate of all the civilized nations!

"Gold! Mr. Oliver, you are indeed a great banker!"

"Oh august majesty! Oh honorable Oliver! Great high priest of gold,

gold, gold! Accept our humble homage and receive our oaths of fealty.

"Yes my friends, gold enough for a continent. But gold is not for circulation. Gold must be hidden. Gold is the soul of healthy money, and a soul is always invisible. But I'll explain all that when you receive your first supply of money.

The secret burial

Before they went their separate ways for the night, Oliver asked them one question.

"How much money will you need to begin with in order to facilitate trading?

They looked at one another then deferentially towards the banker. After a bit of Calculation and with the advice of the kindly financier, thy decided that $200 each would do.

The men parted, exchanging enthusiastic comments. And in spite of the late hour, they spent most of the night lying awake, their imaginations excited by the picture of gold. It was morning before they slept.

As for Oliver, he wasted not a moment. Fatigue was forgotten in the interests of his future as a banker. By dawn's first light he dug a pit into which he rolled the barrel. He then filled it in, transplanting a small shrub to the spot about which he carefully arranged sod. It was well hidden.

Then he went to work with his little press to turn out thousand $1 bills. Watching the clean new banknotes come from the press, the emigrant turned banker, thought to himself:

"My! how simple it is to make money. All its value comes from the products it will buy. Without produce these bills are worthless. My five naïve customers don't realize that. They actually think that this new money derives its value from gold! Their very ignorance makes me their master"

And as evening drew on, the five came to Oliver – on the run.

Who owns the new money!

Five bundles of new banknotes were sitting on the table. "Before distributing the money," said the banker, "I would like your attention."

Now, the basis of all money is gold. And the gold stored away in the vault of my bank is my gold. Consequently, the money is my money. Oh, don't look so discouraged. I'm going to lend you this money and you're going to use it as you see fit. However, you'll have to pay interest. Considering that money is scarce here, I don't think 8% is unreasonable."

"Oh, that's quite reasonable, Mr. Oliver."

"One last point, my friends. Business is business, even between pals. Before you get the money, each of you is going to sign a paper. By it you will bind yourselves to pay both interest and capital under penalty of confiscation of property by me. Oh! this is a mere formality. Your property is of no interest to me. I'm satisfied with money. And I feel sure I'll get my money and that you'll keep your property.

"That makes sense, Mr. Oliver. We're going to work harder than ever in order to pay you back."

"That's the spirit. And any time you have a problem, come and see me. Your banker is your best friend. Now, here's two hundred dollars for each of you"

And our five brave fellows went away, their hands full of dollar bills, their heads swimming with the ecstasy of having money.

A problem in arithmetic

And so Oliver's money went into circulation on the island. Trade, simplified by money, doubled. Everybody was happy and the banker was always greeted with unfailing respect and gratitude.

But now, let's see... Whey does Tom, the prospector, looks so grave as he sits busily figuring with a pencil and paper? It is because Tom, like the others, has signed an agreement to repay Oliver, in one year's time, the $200 plus $16 interest. But Tom has only a few dollars in his pocket and the day of payment is near.

For a long time he wrestled with the problem from his own personal view, without Success. Finally he looked at it from the angle of the little community as a whole.

"Taking into consideration everyone on the island as a whole, he mused, "are we capable of meeting our obligation?" Oliver tuned out a total of $1000. He's asking in return $1080. But even if we bring him every dollar bill on the island, we'll still be $80 short. Nobody made the extra $80. We turn out PRODUCE, not dollar bills. So Oliver can take over the entire island since all the inhabitants together can't Pay him back the total amount of capital and interest. "Even if a few, without any thought for the others, were able to do so, those others would fall. And the turn of the first spared would come eventually. The banker will have everything. We'd better hold a meeting right away and decide what to do about it."

Tom, with his figures in his hand, had no difficulty in proving the situation. All agreed the kindly banker had duped them. They decided upon a meeting at Oliver.

The benevolent banker

Oliver guessed what was on their minds but put up his best front. While he listened, the impetuous Frank stated the case for the group.

"How can we pay you $1080 when there is only $1000 on the entire island?"

"That's is the interest, my friends. Hasn't your rate of production increased?

"Sure, but the money hasn't. And it's money you're asking for, not products. You are the only one who can make money. You've made only $1000 and yet you ask for $1080. That's an impossibility!"

"Now listen, fellows. Bankers, for the greater good of the community, always adapt themselves to the conditions of the time. I'm going to require only the interest. Only $80. You will go on holding the capital."

"Bless you, Mr. Oliver! Are you going to cancel the $200 each of us owes you"?

"Oh no! I'm sorry, but a banker never cancels a debt. You still owe me all the money you borrowed. But you'll pay me, each year, only the interest. If you meet the interest payments faithfully each year I won't push you for the capital. Maybe some won't be able to repay even the interest because of the money changing hands Among you. Well, organize yourselves like a nation. Set up a system of money contributions, what we call taxes. Those who have more money will be taxed more; the poor will pay less. See to it that you bring me, in a lump sum, the total of the amount of interest and I'll be satisfied. And our little nation will thrive."

So our boys left, somewhat pacified but still dubious.

Oliver Glücksterlingmann exults

Oliver is alone. He is deep in reflection. His thoughts run thus:

"Business is good. These boys are good workers, but stupid. Their ignorance and naivety is my strength. They ask for money and I give them the chains of bondage. They give me Orchids and I pick their pockets."

True enough, they could mutiny and throw me into the sea. But pshaw! I have their signatures. They're good Christians. They're honest. They'll honor their pledges. Honest, hardworking people were put in to this world to serve financiers."

"Oh great Rothschild! I feel your banking genius coursing through my entire being! Oh, illustrious master! how right you were when you said :"Give me control of a nation's money and I won't mind who makes its laws." I am the master of Salvation Island because I control its money."

"My soul is drunk with enthusiasm and ambition. I feel I could rule the universe. What I, Oliver Glücksterlingmann, have done here, I can do throughout the entire world. Oh! If only I could get off this island! I know how I could govern the world without wearing a crown.

"My supreme delight would be to instill my philosophy in the mind of those who lead society; bankers, industrialists, politicians, reformers, teachers, journalists, – all would be my servants. The masses are content to live in slavery when the elite from among them are constituted their overseers."

And so the entire philosophy of banking, that spawn of Rothschild, was summed up in this ecstasy of Oliver Glücksterlingmann.

The cost of living unbearable

Meanwhile things went from bad to worse on Salvation Island. Production was up; bartering had dropped to a minimum. Oliver collected his interest regularly.

The others had to think of setting money aside for him. Thus, money tended to clot instead of circulating freely.

Those who paid the most in taxes complained against those who paid less. They raised the prices of their goods to compensate for this loss. The unfortunate poor who paid no taxes lamented the high cost of living and bought less.

If one took a salaried job with another, he was continually demanding increases in salary in order to meet the mounting cost of living.

Morale was low. The joy went out of living. No one took interest in his work. Whey should he? Produce sold poorly. When they made a sale, they had to pay taxes to Oliver. They went without things. It was a real crisis, and they accused one another of wanting in charity and of being the cause of the high cost of living.

One day, Harry, sitting in his orchard, pondered over the situation. He finally arrived at the conclusion that this "progress," born of a refugee's monetary system, had spoiled everything on the island. Unquestionably all five had their faults; but Oliver's system seemed to have been specifically designed to bring out the worst in human nature.

Harry decided to demonstrate this to his friends and to unite them for action. He started with Jim, who was not hard to convince. "I'm no genius," he said, "but for a long time now there's been a bad smell about this foreigner's system".

One by one they came to the same conclusion and ended by deciding upon another conference with Oliver.

Interview with the unshackle

A veritable tempest burst about the ears of the banker.

"Money's scarce on the island, fellow, because you take it away from us! We pay you and pay you and still own you as much as at the beginning. We work our heads off! We've the finest land possible and yet we're worse off than before the day of your arrival. Debts! Debts! up to our necks in debt!"

"Oh! now boys, be reasonable! Your affairs are booming and it's thanks to me. A good banking system is a country's best asset. But if it is to work beneficially, you must have faith in the banker. Come to me as you would to a father... is it more money you want? Very well. My barrel of gold is good for many thousands of dollars more. See, I'm going to mortgage your latest acquisitions and lend you another thousand dollars right now.

"So! Now our debt goes up to $2000! We are going to have twice as much interest to pay for the rest of our lives!"

"Well, yes – but I'll lend you more whenever the value of your property increases.

And you'll never pay anything but the interest. You'll lump all your debts into one what we call consolidated debt. And you can add to the debt year after year.

"And raise the taxes year after year?

"Obviously. But your revenues also increases every year."

"So then, the more the country develops each year because of our labor, the more the public debt increases!"

"Why, of course! Just as in your Canada – or in any other part of the civilized world for that matter. The degree of a country's civilization is always gauged by the size of its debt to the bankers."

"And that's a healthy monetary system, Mr. Oliver?

The wolf devours the lambs

"Gentlemen, all sound money is based on Gold and it comes from the banks in the form of debts. The national debt is a good thing. It keeps men from becoming too satisfied. It subjugates governments to the supreme and ultimate wisdom, that which is incarnate in bankers. As a banker, I am the torch of civilization here on your little island. I will dictate your politics and regulate your standard of living."

"Mr. Oliver, we're simple uneducated folks, but we don't want that kind of civilization here. We'll not borrow another cent off you. Sound money or not, we don't want any further transactions with you."

"Gentlemen, I deeply regret this very ill-advised decision of yours. But if you break with me, remember, I have your signatures. Repay me everything at once – capital and interest."

"But that is impossible, sir. Even if we give you all the money on the island we still won't be square with you."

"I can't help that. Did you or did you not sign? Yes? Very well. By virtue of the sanctity of contracts I hereby seize your mortgaged property, which was what you agreed to at the time, you were so happy to have my help. If you don't want to serve willingly, the supreme authority of money then you'll obey force. You'll continue to exploit the island, but in my interests and under my conditions. now, get out ! You'll get your orders from me tomorrow."

Like Rothschild, Oliver knew that whoever controlled the nation's money, controlled the nation. But he knew also that to maintain that control, it was necessary to keep the people in a state of ignorance and distract them by a variety of means.

Oliver had observed, that of the five islanders, two were conservatives and three were liberals. That much had evolved from their evening conversations, especially after they had fallen into slavery. And between the conservatives and those who were liberals there was constant friction and the two factions wrangled ferociously, forgetting the one who had forged their chains, that money master, the banker Oliver.

On occasions, Harry, the most neutral of the five, considering that all had the same needs and aspirations, had suggested a Union of Electors. Such a union, Oliver could not tolerate; it would mean the end of his rule. No dictator, financial or otherwise, could stand before a people united and educated.

A priceless bit of flotsam

One day, Tom, the prospector, discovered on a small beach hidden by tall grass at one end of the island, a lifeboat, empty except for a trunk in good condition lying in the bottom of it.

He opened the trunk. Among the articles within, a sort of album caught his eye:

"Premiere annee de Vers Demain". Between the covers he found the first volume of a Social Credit publication from Canada.

Tom could read French. Curious, he sat down and began to read the volume. His interest grew; his face lit up.

"Well just look at this "! he cried out loud.

"This is something we should have known a long time ago.

"Money gets its value not from gold, but from the products which that money buys."

"Simply put, money should be a sort of accountancy, credits passing from one account to another according to purchases and sales. The sum total of money will depend upon the sum total of production."

"Each time production increases there is a corresponding increase in the amount of money. Never at any time should interest be paid on new money. Progress is marked, not by an increase in the public debt, but by the issuance of an equal dividend to each individual...Prices are adjusted to the general purchasing power by a coefficient of prices. Social Credit...."

But Tom could no longer contain himself. He got up and set off at a run, his book in his hands, to share this glorious discovery with his four comrades.

Money – elementary accounting

So Tom became the teacher. He thought the others what he had learned from that God-sent Social Credit publication.

"This," he said, "is what we can do without waiting for a banker and his keg of gold or without underwriting a debt."

"I open an account in the name of each of you. In the right hand column are the credits which increase your account; to the left are the debits which subtract from your account."

"Each wants $200 to begin with. Very well. We write $200 to the credit of each. Each immediately has $200.

"Frank buys some goods from Paul to the amount of $10. I deduct $10 from Frank leaving him $190. I add $10 to Paul and he now has $210.

"Jim buys from Paul the amount of $8. I deduct from Jim $8 leaving him $192. Paul now has $218."

"Paul buys wood from Frank for $15. I deduct $15 from Paul leaving him $203.

I add $15 to Frank's account and it goes back to $205."

"And so we continue; from one account to another in the same fashion as paper banknotes go from one man's pocket to another's."

"If someone needs money to expand production, we issue him the necessary amount of new credit. Once he has sold his products, he repays the sum to the "Credit Fund". The same with public works; paid for by new credits."

"Likewise, each one's account is periodically increased but without taking credits from anyone, in order that all may benefit from the progress society makes. That's the "Common Dividend". In this fashion money becomes an instrument of service.

The banker's despair

Everyone understood. The members of this little community became Creditors.

The following day, Oliver, the banker received a letter signed by the five.

"Dear sir, without the slightest necessity you have plunged us into debt and exploited us. We don't need you any more to run our money system. From now on we'll have all the money we need without gold, debts or thieves. We are establishing, at once, the system "Common Dividend" on this island. The common dividend is going to replace the national debt."

"If you insist on being repaid, we can repay you all the money you gave us. But not one cent more. You cannot lay claim to that which you have not made."

"We have nothing against you as a foreigner. We respect every human being. But we reject your mentality and philosophy. And we will not permit anyone to regiment and exploit us."

Oliver was in despair. His empire was crumbling. His dreams shattered. What could he do? Arguments would be futile. The five were now Dividenders; money and credit were not more mysterious to them then they were to Oliver.

"Oh ! esteemed Rothschild ! What will become of your disciple? These men have been won to "Common Dividend. Their doctrine will spread far more quickly than mine. Should I beg forgiveness? become one of them? Financier, a banker and I? Never ! Rather, I shall try and put as much distance between them and me as I can."

Fraud unmasked

To protect themselves against any future claim by Oliver, our five men decided to make him sign a document attesting that he again possessed all he had when he first arrived on the island.

An inventory was taken; the boat, the oars, the little press and the famous barrel of gold.

Oliver had to reveal where he had hidden the gold. Our boys hoisted it from the hole with considerably less respect than the day they had unloaded it from the boat. Common Dividend had taught them to despise of gold.

The prospector, who was helping to lift the barrel, found it surprisingly light for gold. If the barrel was full, he told the others, there was something in it besides gold.

The impetuous Frank didn't waste a moment; a blow of the axe and the contents of the barrel were exposed.

Gold? not so much as a grain of it! Just rocks—plain, worthless rocks!

Our men couldn't get over the shock.

"Don't tell us he could bamboozle us to this extent!"

"Were we such muttonheads as to go into raptures over the mere mention of gold ?"

"Did we mortgage all our possession for a few pieces of paper based on a few pounds of rocks? It's robbery compounded by lies!"

"To think that we sulked and almost hated one another all because of such a fraud! That devil!"

Furious, Frank raised his axe. But already the banker had taken to his legs in full flight towards the forest.

Farewell to Salvation Island

After the opening of the barrel and the revelation of his duplicity, nothing further was heard of Oliver Glücksterlingmann.

Shortly after, a ship, cruising off the normal navigation route, noticed signs of life on this uncharted island and cast anchor a short distance offshore.

The men learned that the ship was en route to America. So they decided to take with them what they could carry and return to Canada.

Above all, they made sure to take back the album "The First Year of Social Creditor (Common Dividend) which had proven to be their salvation from the hands of the financier, Oliver, and which had illumined their minds with an inextinguishable light.

All five solemnly engaged themselves to get in touch with the management of this paper, once back in Canada, and to become devoted and zealous apostles of the cause of Social Credit (Common Dividend) in Canada.

WHY WE DEMAND SOCIAL CREDIT, (SYNONYMOUS WITH "COMMON DIVIDEND) BUT NOT TO BE CONFUSED WITH THE "SOCIAL CREDIT POLITICAL PARTY"

We ask the establishment of Common Dividend in order to free society from financial tyranny.

Farmers have an abundance of food to place on the market. But our existing system of finance doesn't give the consumer sufficient purchasing power to buy, at a reasonable price, the farmer's produce.

We have space, materials and workers to build a solid and specious house for every family. But the present financial regime doesn't place at the disposal of the family the means to pay for the construction of such a house.

Industry finds it hard to keep its products moving; its employees are threatened with unemployment; and all because consumers haven't sufficient money to buy the products of industry.

When the capacity to pay does not conform to the capacity to produce, then finance is out of step with existing possibilities. Produce is easier to come by than money.

Individuals and families are constantly harassed by financial worries and the insecurity of the future. These worries and this insecurity are at complete odds with the realities, which are tremendous; they are a result of the shortage of means to make payments and of the continual threat of losing these means completely.

The soil does not threaten to become sterile; there is no danger of the sun and rain refusing their bounty; nor is laziness on the part of the workers, because their distress is only too evident when they become partially or totally unemployed. The problem is, always and uniquely, one of money.

So then it would seem that the present day system of finance is one prejudicial rather than beneficial to the people.

For this reason, we demand that it be changed in favor of a system, which is one of service, a system of finance proposed by Social Credit (Common Dividend).

Social Credit or Common Dividend makes of money a constant and exact reflection of realities. With the birth of produce, money comes into being; and the total purchasing power of the people is constantly readjusted in order to equal the total sum of produce offered to the people. Furthermore, each citizen receives a monthly dividend in recognition of the fact that each citizen has a right to live and to share in the fruits of progress, which fruits are the heritage passed on by previous generations.

We demand Social Credit or Common Dividend in place of the present false and vicious system because no other financial system has been proposed which serves man in place of tyrannizing him; no other financial system has been proposed which distributes the products of machines as they should be distributed , and guarantees to every individual a share in temporal wealth.

The most urgent and pressing item in any program of temporal reform must be the liberation of society from financial despotism. When this is done, it will be an easy matter to bring an end to the struggle between men to tear from one another the means to go on living; such a struggle is unworthy of intelligent humans in a country where good things are abound, or will be abound, when we have removed that artificial obstacle, the financial obstacle.

A DIVIDEND FOR EVERYONE

Social Creditors or Common Dividenders for that matter, demand a dividend for everyone. This is a sum of money paid periodically to each individual regardless of what revenue his labor brings him. It is exactly like the dividend the capitalist gets even when he is vacationing.

This is a monthly dividend for everyone; for the new-born infant, for the child learning to read, for the adolescent seeking to find himself amid his studies, the young man and woman preparing for the future, for mature man, be he bachelor or breadwinner of a family, for the mother laboring in her home, for the old folks whose thoughts more and more turn towards the homeland awaiting them – to all, to each, from the cradle to the grave.

Canada is a country rich in fertile soil, in forests and running streams and water-power; abounding in minerals of all sorts, rich beyond measure with the techniques of applied science and furnished with industries equipped with the most up-to-date machinery; and, most important of all, endowed beyond words with strong arms, stout hearts and clear minds.

Social Creditors or Common Dividenders for that matter, judge that, in a Canada so richly endowed, it is senseless and idiotic, criminal even, to force multitudes of Canadians to live in constant fear of the morrow, (when it is not a question of worrying for today). Each family, each individual dwelling in this rich land should be guaranteed at least the necessities of life and an easy access to an honest living, not as a privilege, but as just due.

A monthly dividend for everyone; this is the most illuminating economical and political theory that has ever been proposed to a world where the chief problem is not how to get produce but how to distribute it.

From parable to reality

A DEBT MONEY SYSTEM

The debt money system introduced by Oliver into the Salvation Island, made the little community sink into financial debt in proportion as it developed and enriched the island by its own work.

This is exactly what happens in our civilized countries, is it not?

Canada of today is certainly richer, in real wealth, than it was 50, 100 years ago, or in the pioneer's age. But compare the national debt, the sum of all public debts of Canada today with the sum 50,100 Years, three centuries ago!

Yet the Canadians themselves produced this enrichment by their labor and their know how. Then why should they be collectively indebted for the result of their own activities?

As examples, consider the schools, the municipal aqueducts, the bridges, roads and other fabrics of public character. Who build them all? Builders of the country.

Who supplied them with the needed materials? Manufacturers of the country. And how come, they could be employed in public work? Because there were other kinds of workers who produced food, clothes, shoes, which supplied all the things and services required for the wants of the constructors and manufacturers.

Thus the whole population of Canada by its work of different kinds, produced all those developments. If we must obtain goods from abroad, we send other goods abroad in counterpart of them.

Now, what do you see? Everywhere the citizens are taxed to pay those schools, those hospitals, those bridges, roads and other public works. The Canadians, as a collectivity, are compelled to pay what they produced as a collectivity.

You pay the double price

And this is not all. The population is made to pay more than the price of what it produced. Their own production, – a real enrichment – has become for the Canadians a debt burdened with interest. When years are added to years, the sum of the interest can equal or even exceed the amount of the debt imposed by the system. It happens that the population may have to pay two, three times the cost of what its members produced.

In addition to the public debts, there are industrial debts, also loaded with interests. They compel the manufacturers and contractors to increase their prices beyond the cost of production, in order to reimburse the capital and the interests; otherwise they would become insolvent, bankrupt.

Both public and industrial debts are paid, plus interest, by the Canadian population, to the financial system. We pay taxes for the public debts, and a surplus of price for the industrial debts. Prices are swelling while the purse is flattened by taxes.

A tyrannical system

These and many other facts are indicative of a money system, a financial system that controls instead of being a servant; a system to dominate the people—as Oliver dominated the fellows of the Island before they rebelled.

And if the money masters refuse to lend, or if they make their conditions unbearable for the public bodies or for the manufacturers, what happens? It happens that the public bodies give up many projects, no matter how urgent; and the manufactures give up development or production plans that would answer to real need of Canadians. This is a cause of unemployment. And those who have still something, or who earn a salary, must be taxed to prevent the unemployed from starving completely.

Can you imagine a more tyrannical system, with so baneful effects on every Canadian?

A bar to distribution

And this is not all. Not only the money system indebts the producers, or paralyzes the production it refuses to finance, but it is a wretched financial tool for the distribution of the goods.

Notwithstanding the fact that stores, shops and warehouses are full, and everything is at hand for an even greater production, the distribution of the goods already produced is stinted.

You can obtain only what you can pay. In face of an abundant production, there should be an abundance of purchasing power, of money in the wallets of the people.

Such is not the fact. The price of the finished goods is always higher than the amount of money distributed as purchasing power in the course of their production.

This is inherent to the accountancy of the present system of finance, which has no mechanism to fill the gap.

The capacity to pay is not made to equal the capacity to produce. Finance and reality do not work at the same rate. Reality means an abundance of goods easy to produce. Finance means lacking money hard to obtain.

To correct what is wicked

Thus the present money system is truly an oppressive one, when it should be a system of service.

This does not mean that we must do away with it, but we must correct it. The application of the financial principle known as "Social Credit" (synonymous with) "Common Dividend" would make this correction magnificently. (Do not confound Social Credit with the political party, which usurps that name while pursuing other ends and practicing an adverse policy).

The principles of Social Credit, when applied, would make the money system a servant instead of a master. They were discovered and enunciated by C.H. Douglas, (deceased in 1952). His first writings on this subject were published in 1918.

Superpower dominates Governments

BY LOUIS EVEN

Governmental powers

Textbooks generally distinguish three powers belonging to the Government; the legislative, the executive, and the judiciary.

The legitimate and sovereign government of any free country must possess the power to make laws to regulate relationships between citizens and established bodies, without having to ask permission from a foreign authority. This is the exercise of the legislative power.

Likewise, the government of a sovereign country must be able to administer the nation in conformity with the laws and its constitution, without having to submit its action to a foreign government for approval. This is the exercise of the executive power.

Finally, the government of a sovereign country must possess the right to enforce the laws of the country, to prosecute and condemn those who transgress them, to pass judgment on the litigations between citizens throughout the country, without having to request the authority to do so from a foreign government. This is the exercise of the judiciary power.

The Superpower

If these three powers—the legislative, the executive, and the judiciary—are the great constituted powers of any sovereign government, there is another power, not labeled as such, but which exceeds these three powers, and which dominates governments themselves.

This Superpower, which did not receive authority from any constitution, and which does not worry about it, any more then would be a thief in the exercise of his function, is the *"Monetary Power"*

The monetary power is not the money that you have in your wallet. It is neither the stocks nor the bonds that you may have in your portfolio. It is not the taxes that the governments of the three levels—local, provincial, federal—take from you, without ever being satisfied. It is not the pay raise, for which the trade unions yell, and over which they declare strikes. It is not even the industrial dividends that some Socialists would like to take away from Capitalists and to see distributed to wage earners, without having calculated the insignificant drop that each one would get from them. The monetary power is not what some governments call inflation, and what some employees call a rise in the standard of living, while governments and trade unions contribute to inflation as much as they can, the former by their ever-increasing taxes the latter by their demands for wage or salary increases.

No, all this is small stuff compared to the stature and the power of the Superpower that we are denouncing, this power that can make our lives "hard, cruel, and relentless".

This power becomes particularly irresistible when exercised by those who, because they hold and control money, are able also to govern credit and determine it allotment, for that reason supplying, so to speak, the life-blood to the entire economic body, and grasping, as it were, in their hands the very soul of production. so that no one dare to breathe against their will.

These strong words may look immoderate to those who are unaware, on the one hand, of the role of money and credit in economic life, and on the other hand, of control to which money and credit are subjected.

The Blood of economic life

Let us recall immediately, without explaining it here, that financial credit has the same virtue as cash in economies life. One buys materials, services, work, products, as much with cheques' – which simply transfer figures from one account to another in bank ledgers – as with coins or paper money, which go from a client to the local retailer at the corner store. It is the money of figures (cheques) that activates the more economic life, being responsible for more then 80 percent of the total financial operations of our nation's commerce and industry. The generic term "money" can therefore refer to both forms of means of payment.

Above Governments

Monetary power is the power of issuing the nation's money and credit; the power of conditioning the putting of money and credit into circulation; the power of determining the length of time of circulation of this financial credit; the power of demanding the return of money at a term fixed beforehand, on pain of confiscation of goods, which are the fruit of the labor of those being subjected to confiscation; the power of bringing governments into subjection, of fixing for them also the conditions of its release and of its return, of demanding as a guarantee the power that all governments have of taxing their citizens.

Now, this financial credit, this money, is the permission to make use of the production capacity, not of the controllers, but of the country's population. The controllers of money and credit do not cause a single stalk of wheat to grow, do not produce one pair of shoes, do not manufacture one sole brick, do not dig into a mine shaft, do not pave one square inch of road. It is the country's population that carries out these projects. It is therefore its own real credit. But to be able to use it, one needs the approval of the controllers of money, of the financial credit, which is nothing more than the registering of figures in the banks ledgers, representing the value of the nation's real credit.

The banker's pen which consents or refuses to give to individuals, to corporations, to governments, the right to mobilize the skills of professionals, the nation's natural resources, that pen commands; it grants or refuses; it sets conditions on the financial permits that it gives; it puts into debt those individuals or governments to whom it grants permits. The banker's pen has the power of a scepter in the hands of a superpower – the monetary power.

We endured ten years of economic paralysis. Not one government thought it had the power to put an end to it. A declaration of ware came, and the financial permits to produce, draft, to destroy and to kill, suddenly appeared overnight.

A diabolical monstrosity

There is not a worse tyranny than that of the monetary power: a tyranny which makes itself felt in all homes, in all institutions, in all public administrations, in all governments.

And from whence does this superpower take its authority? The other three government powers obtain their authority from their country's Constitution. But what constitution was able to give to a superpower the right to hold government's themselves under its thumb?

The fact that these same states of affairs exist in all developed countries does not justify this monstrosity. It only goes to show that the superpower of money and credit holds the entire civilized world in its tentacles. This makes it even more diabolical.

Yes, it is a diabolical power, but which took on a sacred aura, to such an extent that one looked for the causes of our economic and social woes everywhere, except in the operation of the money and credit system. It is permitted to look somewhere else; but in the monetary system, that is not permitted, not even for the sovereign governments.

A CONSTITUTIONAL MONETARY POWER

What is needed in its stead is a monetary power, established by constitution or by law, in order to make of the monetary organism an organism at the service of the community, as are the other three services mentioned above.

What is needed is a monetary power exercised by an organism similar to the judiciary system, staffed with qualified accountants, instead of judges, fulfill their duties independently of powers to be.

If the pen of an usurped superpower can create or refuse, according to the will of this tyrant, the financial credit, based on the nation's real credit, the pen from a "Constitutional Monetary Power" would be as effective to issue the financial credit, to the service of the population, of all the members of society. This end would be specified in the law.

There would no longer be purely financial hindrances. Getting in to debt to foreign bankers for things that we can produce in our own country – this preposterousness would cease to exist. Prices going up, when production becomes easier and more plentiful – such an inconsistency would cease to exist in a monetary body obligated, by law, to make of the financial aspects of the economy the exact reflection of reality. The seeking of new job creations while the machine, instead of human labor, supplies products – such a ridiculous policy would be relegated to a past history of subjection to a monster. The astronomical waste, due to the production of things useless to the normal needs of the people, with the sole end of creating jobs, would be banned as a lack of responsibility to the generations, which must succeed us.

And thousands of other things as well will follow with the establishment of a constitutional monetary power of service, and with the doing away with the unbearable rule that wants to link income solely to employment, when the first effect of progress should be to free man from economic tasks in order to allow to freely devote himself to activities which are less materialistic, and to tend towards the blossoming out of his personality and freedom.

ABRAHAM LINCOLN AND JOHN F. KENNEDY

Two great presidents of the United States
Assassinated for the cause of justice

BY MELVIN SICKLER

November 22,2003 marks the 40 the anniversary of the assassination of U.S. president John F. Kennedy, and a majority of Americans still believe that there was a conspiracy behind this assassination. Both Abraham Lincoln and Kennedy were assassinated while they held the high office of President of the United States. Both of these former presidents had also created their own money system to run the United States while they were in office. Is this just a coincidence?

Why assassinate a President? Why must everything be kept so covered up? What are they trying to hide from the American people? The facts will speak for themselves.

During the Civil Ware (1861 – 1865), President Lincoln needed money to finance the War from the North. The bankers were going to charge him 24% to 36% interest. Lincoln was horrified and went away greatly distressed, for he was a man of principle and would not think of plunging his beloved country into a debt that the country would find impossible to pay back.

Eventually President Lincoln was advised to get Congress to pass a law authorizing the printing of full legal tender Treasury notes to pay for the war effort. Lincoln recognized the great benefits of this issue. At one point he wrote:

"...(we) gave the people of this Republic the greatest blessing they have ever had—their own paper money to pay their own debts..."

The Treasury notes were printed with green ink on the back, so the people called them "Greenbacks".

Lincoln printed 400 million dollars worth of Greenbacks (the exact amount being $449,338,902), money that he delegated to be created, a debt-free and interest-free money to finance the war. It served as legal tender for all debts, public and private.

He printed it, paid to the soldiers, the U.S. Civil Service employees, and bought supplies for the war.

Shortly after that happened, "The London times" printed the following: "If the mischievous financial policy, which had its origin in the North American Republic, should become indurate down to a fixture, then that Government will furnish its own money without cost. It will pay off debts and be without a debt. It will have all the money necessary to carry on its commerce. It will become prosperous beyond precedent in the history of the civilized governments of the world. The brains and the wealth of all countries will go to North America. That government must be destroyed, or it will destroy every monarchy on the globe.

The Bankers obviously understood. The only thing, I repeat, the only thing that is a threat to their power is sovereign government printing interest free and debt free paper money. They know it would break the power of the international Bankers.

In retaliation

After this was published in "The London Times," the British Government, which was controlled by the London and other European Bankers, moved to support the Confederate South, hoping to defeat Lincoln and the Union, and destroy this government, which they said had to be destroyed.

Two things stopped them. First, Lincoln knew the British people, and he knew that Britain would not support slavery, so he issued the Emancipation Proclamation, which declared that slavery in the United States was abolished. At this point, the Londoner Bankers could not openly support the Confederacy because the British people simply would not stand for their country supporting slavery.

Second, the Czar of Russia sent a portion of the Russian navy to the United States with orders that its admiral would operate under the command of Abraham Lincoln. These ships of the Russian navy then became a threat to the ships of the British navy, which had intended to break the blockade and help the South.

The North won the war and the Union was preserved. America remained as one nation.

Of course, the bankers were not going to give in that easy, for they were determined to put an end to Lincoln's interest free, debt free, Greenbacks. An agent of the Bankers assassinated him shortly after the war ended.

Thereafter, Congress revoked the Greenback Law and enacted, in its place, the National Banking Act. The national Banks were to be privately owned and the national bank notes they issued were to be interest bearing. The Act also provided that the Greenbacks should be retired from circulation as soon as they came back to the Treasury in payment of taxes.

In 1972, the United States Treasury Department was asked to compute the amount of interest that would have been paid if those 400 million dollars had been borrowed at interest instead of being issued by Abraham Lincoln. They did some computation, and a few weeks later, the United State Treasury Department said the United States Government saved 4 billion dollars in interest because Lincoln had created his own money. So you can about imagine how much the Government has paid and how much we owe solely on the basis of interest.

The Federal Reserve Act

There were changes in the money and banking laws for the next fifty years. Finally in 1913, the Bankers were able to get their Federal Reserve Act passed through Congress, which replaced the National Banking Act that had earlier replaced the Greenback Law. If the Government would have continued the policy of Abraham Lincoln, the warnings given in "The London Times" would have come to pass. America would be a debt-free nation, the most prosperous in the world. And the brains and the wealth of the world would have come to America.

But with this Federal Reserve Act being passed, Congress gave up its power to create its own money that it was given in the United States Constitution, and gave this power over to private Bankers who called themselves the Federal Reserve. The bankers had achieved their ultimate goal, for now the United States operated under a central bank that was privately owned. They now had the power to run the country by controlling the creation of the money, and were free to charge the interest they so desired.

As Maier Anselm Rothschild once said: "Permit me to issue and control the money of a nation, and I care not who makes its laws..."

No United States president since Abraham Lincoln dared to go against the system and create his own money, as many of these so called elected presidents were actually only instruments or puppets of the bankers. That is until President John F. Kennedy came into office.

President Kennedy was not afraid to "buck the system," for he understood how the Federal Reserve System was being used to destroy the United States. As a just and honorable man, he could not tolerate such a system, for it smelled corruption from A to Z. Certainly he must have known about the Greenbacks, which Abraham Lincoln created when he was in office.

On June 4th, 1963, President Kennedy signed a presidential document, called Executive Order 111 10, which further amended Executive Order

10289 of September 19th, 1951. This gave Kennedy, as President of the United States, legal clearance to create his own money to run the country, money that would belong to the people, an interest and debt-free money. He had printed United States Notes, completely ignoring the Federal Reserve Notes from the private banks of the Federal Reserve.

Our records show that Kennedy issued $4,292,893,825 of cash money. It was perfectly obvious that Kennedy was out to undermine the Federal Reserve System of the United States.

But it was only a few months later, in November of 1963, that the world received the shocking news of President Kennedy's assassination. No reason was given, of course, for anyone wanting to commit such an atrocious crime. But for those who knew anything about money and banking, it did not take long to put the pieces of the puzzle together. For surely, President Kennedy must have had in mind to repeal the Federal Reserve Act of 1913, and turn back to the United States Congress the power to create its own money.

It is interesting to note that, only one day after Kennedy's assassination, all the United States notes, which Kennedy had issued, were called out of circulation. Was this through an executive order of the newly installed president, Lyndon B. Johnson? Was President Johnson afraid of the bankers? Or was he one of their instrument? At any rate, all of the money President Kennedy had created was destroyed.

And not a word was said to the American people.

A LESSON TO LEARN

There is much that can be learned from our past history. Here we are in 2003, and the United States is still operating under the "Federal Reserve System". It has already plunged this country over 6.9 trillion dollars in debt – Federal debt, (the total debt, including that of individuals and corporations, is over 43 trillions) a debt it will never be able to pay, and has been responsible for every kind of corruption imaginable. Yet barely a peep of protest can be heard from the American people.

All the Bankers have to do to keep their power, is to get rid of the few politicians who are honestly working for a reform in our economic system, and the people at large remain ignorant and controlled. It is obvious, the American people need to be awakened to the truth.

The population at large must be educated on the "Federal Reserve," and then unite together to put pressure on the Government to get the "Federal Reserve Act of 1913" repealed. Otherwise, it will spell disaster for the United States.

Abraham Lincoln and John F. Kennedy both had the courage to stand up for principles and to fight for justice. They have both gone down in history as being true patriots of the United States. But do we, as citizens, have the courage to follow their example? Melvin Sickler

Quotes on money

"The bank hath benefit of interest on all money which it creates out of nothing."

William Paterson, founder of the Bank of England, 1694.

"All the perplexities, confusion and distresses in America arise not from defects in the constitution or confederation, nor from want of honor or virtue, as much from downright ignorance of the nature of coin, credit, and circulation."

John Adams, letter to Thomas Jefferson.

If congress has the right under the Constitution to issue paper money, it was given them to use themselves, not to be delegated to individuals or corporations.

US President Andrew Jackson.

"The Government should create, issue. and circulate all the currency and credits needed to satisfy the spending power of the Government and the buying power of the consumers. By the adoption of these principles, the taxpayers will be saved immense sums of interest. Money will be ceasing to be master and become the servant of humanity."

US President Abraham Lincoln.

"History records that the money changers have used every form of abuse, intrigue, deceit, and violent means possible to maintain their control over governments by controlling money and its issuance."

US President James Madison.

"The money power denounces, as public enemies, all who question its methods or throw light upon its crimes."

Democrat Presidential candidate William Jennings Bryan.

"Whoever controls the volume of money in any country is absolute master of all industry and commerce."

US President James A. Garfield.

"This Federal Reserve Act establishes the most gigantic trust on earth. When the President (Wilson) signs this bill, the invisible government of the Monetary Power will be legalized."

Hon. Charles A. Lindbergh.Sr.

"Bankers own the earth; take it away from them but leave them with the power to create credit; and, with a flick of a pen, they will create enough money to bay it back again... If you want to be slaves of bankers and pay the cost of your own slavery, then let the bankers control money and control credit."

Sir Josiah Stamp, Director, Bank of England. 1940.

"Banks lend by creating credit. They create the means of payment out of nothing."

Ralph M. Hawtrey, former Secretary of Treasury, England.

"The banks do create money. They have been doing it for a long time, but they didn't quite realize it, and they did not admit it. Very few did. You will find it in all sorts of documents, financial text books. etc. But in the intervening years, and we must all be perfectly frank about these things, there has been a development of thought, until today very much whether you would get many prominent bankers to attempt to deny that banks create credit."

H.W. White, Chairman of the Associated banks of New Zealand, to the New Zealand Monetary Commission, 1955.

Thoughts about Unemployment or War

C.H. DOUGLAS

Now, that is whey you have all this careful suggestion that what we want is a reduction of unemployment, and we are so badly trained in the nature of the possibilities of democratic government, that we say, "Yes, what we want is a reduction of unemployment." Yet the urge towards a reduction of unemployment is the direct cause of the coming war. The moment you say you must have everybody employed, you have to find somewhere to which the goods you produce can go—the goods that you cannot use yourselves. You must find export markets, and the competition for export markets is the direct cause of war.

You are right in saying, "We want the disappearance of these terrible things, these depressions which accompany unemployment," but you are not right when you say that we want the abolition of unemployment, because with the abolition of unemployment, as things now are, you get something you do not want, which is war. That is only one—but a very fundamental one—of the reasons why it is essential that you should get control of your Members of Parliament.

The process of increasing the productive efficiency of human labor, and of gradually diminishing the amount of it required—and of supplementing it by saving machinery, during the past 150 years, has now reached the stage at which society, if so organized, can make available an ample sufficiency of the material necessities of life for all with a steadily diminishing amount of human labor.

Which means, less hour work per day and less days per week, without a diminishing in the standard of living.

The Nature of Credit, Sacred and Profane

T.V. HOLMES, M.A., LL.B.

There was a time, not so long ago, when Money was Gold, or supposed to be Gold, and for that reason carried worldwide authority. But this delusion was destroyed in 1914 at the outbreak of World War I. The Banks then confessed themselves unable to carry out their obligation to repay their clients' bank deposits in Gold. The Banks were to all intents and purposes "bankrupt". Only the action of the Government in printing "Treasury Notes" and forcing the Banks depositors to accept these Notes in lieu of "Gold Sovereigns" saved the Banks and the whole Banking System from "bankruptcy." Not that the "Treasury Notes" were allowed to indefinitely in circulation. The Banks had no desire to see State Credit tokens substituted for Bank Credit tokens. Sometime in the 1920s the State gave up its right to issue "Treasury Notes" and once again the "Bank of England Note" enjoyed monopoly status.

And ever since 1914 it has been an offence for an individual to possess or horde "Gold Sovereigns." Ever since 1914 Bank Credits has had to be accepted by the community as a sufficient Financial Credit. Ever since 1914 the nation's Financial Credit has been the property and monopoly of the Banking System.

The basic nature of Money

Money has no reality in itself. That in itself it is gold, silver, nickel, copper, cowry shells, or broken teacups. The thing, which makes it money, no matter of what it is made, is purely psychological, and consequently there is no limit to the amount of money except a psychological limit.

What Do We Mean By Real Common Dividend?

(Synonymous with Social Credit)

LOUIS EVEN

Above political parties

Contrary to too widespread an idea in Canada, what we mean with "Social Credit" should not to be confused and is not a political party.

Social Credit is a doctrine, a series of principles expressed for the first time by Major and engineer C. H. Douglas in 1918. The implementation of these principles would make the social and economic organism effectively reach its proper end, which is the service of human needs.

Social Credit would neither create the goods nor the needs, but it would eliminate any artificial obstacle between the two of them, between production and consumption, between the wheat in elevators and the bread on the table. The obstacle today—at least in the developed countries—is purely of financial order, a money obstacle. Now, the financial system neither proceeds from God nor nature. Established by men, it can be adjusted to serve men and no more to cause them problems.

To this end, Social Credit presents concrete propositions. Though very simple, these propositions nevertheless imply a real revolution. Social Credit brings the vision of a new civilization, if by civilization one can mean man's relationship with his fellow men and the conditions of life making easier, for each one the blossoming of his personality.

Under a Social Credit system, we would no longer be struggling with problems that are strictly financial, which constantly plague public administrations, institutions, families, and which poison relationships between individuals. Finance would be nothing but an accounting system, expressing in figures the relative values of goods and services, making easier the mobilization and coordination of the energies required for the different levels of production towards the finished good, and distributing to ALL consumers the means to choose freely and individually what is suitable to them among the goods offered or immediately realizable.

For the first time in history, absolute economic security, without restrictive conditions, would be guaranteed to each and everyone. Material poverty would be a thing of the past. Material anxiety about tomorrow would disappear. Bread would be ensured to all, as long as there is enough wheat to make enough bread. Similarly for the other goods that are necessary for life.

Each citizen would be presented with this economic security as a birthright, as a member of the community, usufructuary throughout one's life of an immense community capital that has become a dominant factor of modern production. This capital is made up of, among other things, the natural resources, which are a collective good; life in society, with the increment that ensues from it; the sum of the discoveries, inventions, technological progress, which are an ever-increasing heritage from generations.

This community capital, which is so productive, would bring each of its co-owners, each citizen, a periodical dividend, from the cradle to the grave. And seeing the volume of production attributable to the common capital, the dividend to each one aught to be at least sufficient to cover the basic necessities of life. This dividend would be given in addition to those who personally take part in production, without prejudice to wages, salaries or other forms of reward.

An income thus attached to the individual, and no longer only attached to his status of employee, would shield him from exploitation by other human beings. With the basic necessities of life guaranteed, a man can better resist being pushed about and can better take up the career of his own choosing.

That is why Social Credit cannot be achieved from a simple change of a party in power to one other. One must make it known, make it wanted, make it sought after by the population, win people over to a standpoint favorable to the vision presented by Social Credit.

Therefore the problem is not of boosting a political party, but of making Social Credit known, loved and wanted. And if this desire is strong enough, this concentrated will of the people has to be brought to the attention to the government. If this doesn't show results ore it is reluctant to act, then there should be a referendum demanded by the population, to force the government to change the constitution and add to its powers, "Legislative, Executive and Judiciary" also the "Monetary" power, which has to be taken from the banks and operated according to the principles of "Social Credit" Of course that could become a deadly undertaking, see President "Abraham Lincoln" and "J.F. Kennedy"

Besides, the very conception of a party is at variance with the philosophy of Social Credit. Political parties exist to try to take power, and are on the move only when the race for power is opened. As for Social Credit, it would distribute power as widely as possible among all members of society by making the Members of Parliament the real representatives of their constituents, and no more the servants of a party.

It is a must for the electorate to learn to express their common will at all times. The decisions affecting the lives of the citizens are made between elections. To content oneself with voting for a party candidate, then to passively accept anything, which is decided upon without the advice from those who must bear the cost of decisions, is political childishness.

Objection: Gold

—But we must have gold as a basis for our money!

—Money gets its value from production and mutual confidence. Empty Canada of all useful production : it becomes a real desert. Of what use would money be, even in gold? On the contrary, leave Canada just as it is, with all kinds of possible production, and suppose it to have a corresponding amount of money, in paper or merely as figures in a ledger, this money would certainly be accepted everywhere and serve to purchase useful things.

—But then what about the gold standard?

—The gold standard is a definition of the monetary unit of each country, formulated to allow comparisons between the monies of different countries. If you say that the Canadian dollar is worth 40 grains of gold, it means that you get, for a Canadian dollar, 40 grains of gold or the equivalent in merchandise. Even if the gold is not there, if the goods are there, you can still get them for your dollar.

—But money not backed by gold, will it be good abroad?

—Money is a national matter. The Canadian dollar does not circulate in

France, nor does the French France circulate in Canada. The French buyers or retailers do not ask themselves if Canada has many or a few Dollars in circulation. What interests them is how much one dollar can buy.

Since May 1. 1940, the Bank of Canada does not own any more gold to back up its notes : is the Dollar less good than it was on April 30. 1940?

The gold myth is a fetish that the masters of money and credit keep alive so as to carry out their plans more easily. Isn't it rather silly to condition a man's right to eat by the amount of gold in existence rather than by the amount of food available? and similarly for the other goods?

Objections: laziness

—Social Credit will make people lazy.

—Why?

—Because it wants to increase the amount of money, And money makes people lazy.

—It is precisely when there is money in circulation that goods sell; and it is when goods sell that industry is able to supply work to employees. It is not work, but condemnation to inactivity, which tends to make a man lazy.

Moreover, laziness is a vice—one of the seven deadly sins. It is not through financial means that one corrects vices. It is not the role of finance to take the place of education, morals, prayers, the sacraments, and religion.

—Yes, but this money for nothing, and guaranteed to everyone!

—It is not money for nothing. It is an income from a capital that belongs to everyone. And it is money to buy available goods.

The assurance of a minimum income, instead of making man lazy, places him in a position where he is able to select a line of work in accord with his taste and ability, which ultimately works to the greater good of the community.

There are no better workers than those who work at a job they like, a job of their own choosing; not hard labor, not a career imposed dictatorially, but a work freely chosen.

The dividend makes up purchasing power to buy products. Therefore it implies the work of men and machines to meet this demand. It is obvious that if production stops, no amount of money can be considered purchasing power, since their will be nothing to buy. The creation of money under such circumstances would not at all be the reflection of realities. Social Credit works according to realities.

The dividend to all would be, like the wages and salaries of the workers, a stimulant to production, since it would grow with production.

The dividend to all would not do away with the wages and salaries of those people employed in production. There would still be same difference between a man having only the dividend and a man having dividend and salary.

Objection: Communism

—Giving everyone the same amount of money will place everybody on equal footing; that's Communism!

—The dividend will not even out fortunes. Peter has $100,000. Paul has $100. If I give each of them $40, will they be equally wealthy? Each is better off than he was before, but the poor man feels the improvement more.

—Something for nothing, that's Communism!

—Not at all. What does Communism want? When Communism demands an economic lot equal for all, that has been proofed wrong! (see former U.D.S.S.R). But when we ask for each human being the right to the basic necessities of life, because

God created material goods for the whole of the human species, this is not Communism but Christian sociology. It is the law of "usus commonis", stating the right of every human being to the use of temporal wealth. If the Communists recall it to a world, which has forgotten it, they are right. The other law, that of private property, is also just, and the Capitalists are right to hold on to it, just as the Communists are wrong to deny it.

Social Credit, wants the observation of both laws. Social Credit, by its dividend to all, suggests a method to legally guarantee to each one a minimum share of the goods created for all men. By balancing global purchasing power with prices, it makes the selling of production easier and thus consolidates private property.

Communism wants to enslave everybody to the State. Contrary to it, Social Credit, by guaranteeing a vital minimum to all, allows them to find jobs in accordance with their aptitudes; in making production profitable, it frees the citizens from continual recourse to the state's intervention and its grant, which make freedom waver.

Opposition: where and why?

Are there people opposed to Social Credit? (Common Dividend).

Yes indeed, and here are some types of these adversaries.

The big shots at the head of the banks and the trust companies formed about the banks, are opposed to Social Credit. They see it as an end to their precious monopoly and their exploitation of the public.

Their political servants, who are more sensitive to the electoral funds than to the public's needs, support the banker's opposition. The political parties have not yet made Social Credit an integral part of their programs, precisely because they listen only to the voices of those supplying them with money, and because the body of the citizens, insufficiently informed, has not yet made its voice heard.

The distributors of patronage are generally opposed to Social Credit; if the public has money, they will have no importance any more.

Certain of the newly rich are opposed to Social Credit because they like to stand out by eclipsing those who have nothing. They fear that once the public has no more the need to crawl for the right to live, it will begin to judge men by their moral qualities and not by the size of their wallets.

Ignorant people of various types are opposed to Social Credit. Some know nothing at all about Social Credit, yet condemn it from stupidity or prejudice. Others interpret it wrongly and imagine that their fortunes will be confiscated. Others believe that people must be poor to behave properly; they acknowledge that they themselves are quite capable of making proper use of money, but they look upon their neighbors as professional sinners and find that the bankers help human beings in their salvation by keeping them poor! There are still others who are so married to their own pet beliefs that they refuse, either through pride or narrow-mindedness, to believe that these beliefs can have any merit.

Note that the opponents affirm or deny, but offer no proofs. Or they do so by distorting Social Credit so as to be able to attack it.

Today, money comes into existence in a ledger as a debt owed by man.

Money at its birth, is master. Man, on the other hand, is born indebted to finance. He comes into this world as a slave of money.

Under a Social Credit system, money would still originate from a ledger, but whit-out bearing interest and therefore serving each citizen instead of enslaving them.

Each child would be born with the right to a dividend; money would therefore serve him immediately.

Being considered just as a symbol to represent wealth, and a claim on goods, money would be the exact reflection of wealth, of the available useful things. For production requiring human labor, money would come through wages and salaries; for easy production, easy money; abundant production, abandoned money; automatic production, free money; for production increased by a common capital, trough the factor of organized society, money issued by a "SOCIAL SOURCE" and distributed to each and everyone.

Various Excerpts from the Social Creditor in Front of an Election

Any Social Creditor, even slightly informed, knows very well that today, the supreme power is exercised neither by the people nor by their government but by a financial clique. Statesman like Gladstone, Wilson and many others, declared it explicitly. Mackenzie King was promising, in 1935, the greatest battle of all times "between the financial powers and the people." A battle in which he did not engage, no doubt because he considered the financial powers too strong and the people to weak.

Social Credit will enter into the country's legislation when it will have become the object of a general request, asserted so much that all political parties will welcome it into their programs. To confine it into a political party is to link its fate to the electoral fate of the party.

One must build up the people's strength, so that their weight on the governments exceeds the strength of the financial powers. It is not in a parliament that one builds up the people's strength. It is where the people are—outside of parliaments. And it is the place of a true Social Credit Movement.

The only strength capable of effectively putting this pressure is the strength of an informed, united and determined people that imperatively requests result. Who can build up such strength? Those who are working at it, the active Social Creditors. Where can they build it up? Outside of Parliament, since it is outside of the Parliament that the people are.

A "PARTY", THE OPPOSITE OF SOCIAL CREDIT

(TAKEN FROM "VERS DEMAIN" JANUARY 15. 1962)

A true Social Creditor cannot be a party man. Party und Social Credit are two terms, which exclude one another, by their very nature and definition.

Thirst for power

A political party organizes a group around politicians to try to come to power.

Social Credit views power redistributed to the individuals: economic power, by the guarantee of a dividend allowing each individual to order from production the goods he needs; political power, in making the State the property of the individuals, instead of the individuals the property of the State.

The party system leads the citizens to put their confidence in a group of politicians. Social Credit teaches the citizens to take on their responsibilities and in politics, to make themselves the governments' supervisors and conscience.

A political party divides the people, by forming a group to struggle against other groups that seek the same power; and any division weakens. Social Credit unites the citizens around common, fundamental aspirations, and invites them to unite their demands so that the governments may implement these demands, whatever the party in power. If the people are not strong enough to put a government at the service, it is not the government that must be changed, but the people that must be made more powerful; this certainly cannot be achieved by dividing, but by uniting.

With power, constraint

A political party wants power, therefore the right to use force, because power is exercised by administrative, legislative, executive measures, which compel under fear of punishment. It is the opposite of Social Credit, which loathes compulsion, and advocates inducement. Social Credit loathes what is compulsory, and stands for freedom of choice; now, everything, which comes from the government, is compulsory.

The Social Creditor who pledges allegiance to a party, of whatever domination, for the conquest of power shows by this, that he is not really a Social Creditor, even if he bears the name and even though he would know the monetary proposition of Social Credit very well. He is somewhat like a Christian who, while knowing the teaching of the Gospel very well, even to the point of being able to present them to others, would behave according to a spirit exactly contrary to it.

FOR A POWERFUL PEOPLE

If you elect a Social Credit party, supposing you could, I may say that I regard the election of a Social Credit party in this country as one of the greatest catastrophe that could happen."

The financial power did not come about suddenly, and it will not disappear suddenly. It is firm established today; and it is certainly not X's written on ballots every three, four or five years that will dislodge it from its entrenchments. Only one strength can face it: that of a whole people, of a people sufficiently informed and united to demand the change that is essential in the financial system.

These criticisms should not be taken as directed against bank employees; not even against bank managers and inspectors. They are but workers like you and me, from who are required complex precision, irreproachable integrity, proper dress, constant courtesy, and perfect obedience. It is the system that is at fault, and the banks employees are the first ones to suffer the consequences.

PRESENT TAXES ARE A ROBBERY

New money from Gilberte Côte-Mercier

Q.—How do you want the government to pay for its roads?

A.—The government must pay for its roads with new money, created by a "Credit Office" at the same time as the road is created. The engineers and workers build the road. The financiers must create the credit, the money to pay for the road, as the road is built. They must create as much money as required. Brand new money, since it is a new road. Money taken from nowhere, neither from taxpayer's pockets nor elsewhere. Money specially created for the road. For a new production, newly created money. New money for a new road. As you can see, the road is not paid for with taxes, but with new credit, since credit is money.

Q.—Yes, but if the "Credit Office" thus always creates new money for all public services, there will be a lot of new money! Will this not cause inflation?

A.—The "Credit Office" must create money for production that is being made and destroy money for consumption and wear. This "National Credit Office" keeps the national accounts. It keeps the accounts of production and consumption, which is made up of the use of material goods and labor, and the wear of things. The "Credit Office" creates money for production and destroys it for consumption. It creates it as production is made and destroys it as production is consumed. In this manner, there is a constant balance between the prices of goods and purchasing power.

With this balance, individuals are provided with all the necessary money to pay for all private and public services.

Q.—Do you mean the "Credit Office" must also create the money for private production?

A.—Most certainly. The "Credit Office" must create the money for all production, private and public. The money created for private production is distributed to individuals through three channels: finance without interest to private enterprises; the discount on prices, given to buyers; and the dividend given to all citizens. And the money created for public production is handed to the governments for public services. This is how taxes disappear. Also disappearing is the largest part of the taxes, the part that is presently used to pay the interest on public loans and to repay the borrowed principal. The national debt will no longer exist, and consequently, there will be no more need to service that debt. Taxes will be lowered accordingly.

Q.—But, then, do you mean there were will still be some taxes to pay?

A.—Services like garbage collection and firemen will still be paid for by taxpayers. But the "Credit Office" must distribute to the individuals all the required money to pay for all public and private services. Service must be paid for with money. Money is an accounting system. Accounting must never lack in front of offered services. The "Credit Office" must include in its accounting this real wealth represented by our firemen. And the "Credit Office" must make sure that the population has the required money to pay the firemen. The same for the private sector. There is as much butter for sale as the population can consume. Butter is the true wealth , the real wealth. The financial wealth, the money wealth, the money is only an accounting figure. The "National Credit Office" must make sure that the individuals do not lack money to pay for butter.

The part played by the "Credit Office" is to supply money to the country, just as the farmer's part is to supply food to the country. If the farmers do not need a lot of persuading to do their part, why should the "Credit Office"? Today, the "Credit Office" is not a national office but an office of private individuals. It is the banks, which exist for the profit of the bankers; instead of a true "Credit Office", well kept, that would exist for the whole population. It would be a national or provincial "Credit Office": A "Quebec Credit Office" an "Ontario Credit Office", etc.

Q.—So we must absolutely have a "National or Provincial Credit Office"!

A.—Certainly. Without a "National Credit Office," it would be anarchy in the money system, in our family budgets and in the government's budgets. Taxes are a robbery. The whole present financial system is a robbery from A to Z. This is well explained in the "Michael" Journals and we have good booklets that throw light on the great wonder of the technique of "Social Credit" or its equivalent "Common Dividend"

80% OF YOUR INCOME TAX
GOES TO PAY THE INTEREST ON
THE NATIONAL DEBT

If a social organism created money on behalf of society, for the needs of society, and according to the wealth of society, there would be no more national debt and consequently, no income tax to pay.

The richest countries in the world are the most debt-ridden one. It is nonsense.

In April, 1990, the United States public debt was 3 trillion dollars.

In March, 1990, Canada's debt was 351 billion dollars ($113 million per day in interest) And it is the same thing in all the countries. Third world countries are so indebted to the banks that they cannot even pay the interest on their debts.

There is only one solution to write off the national debt of all the countries, for it is the greatest swindle of all times. Countries should create their own money instead of borrowing it from the banks.

Guernsey's monetary experiment

BY LOUIS EVEN

Guernsey is a small island located in the English Channel. An Anglo-Norman population. This island is located closer to the French coast than to the English one.

At the close of the Napoleonic wars, the island, like several other countries, was in pitiful condition, both physically and financially.

No Money

Sea walls, roads, markets were needed. There was no manpower shortage. But there was no money to pay for these works.

The money used by the people on the Island was the money from England, the pound sterling. But, like after any other war, the financiers were calling back the money advanced to finance the slaughter, and the pounds sterling were very scarce everywhere.

The Island had an autonomous government. "the States of Guernsey." So it had the rights inherent in all sovereign governments, among other rights, that of regulating the volume of money in circulation in the country. But, no more than any other country, the States of Guernsey had thought of exercising this sovereign prerogative.

An intelligent Governor

The Island was especially in need of a new Market House, and a Committee was set up to take care of it. The Committee went to see the Governor to explain the situation to him:

—"We need a new Market, but we have no money to build it."

—"With what material are you going to build a Market?" asked the Governor.

—"With stone and wood."

—"Do you have it in the island?"

—"Certainly, and in plenty."

—"Do you have workers?"

—"Yes again. But it is money that is lacking."

—"Could not your Parliament issue the money?" asked the Governor.

A new idea!

This idea had never occurred to the Committeemen, who had never analyzed the money question. They knew where to get money when there was some, but they never wondered where money begins or can begin.

The method of taxing when there was money was quite familiar. But the method of injecting the money that is lacking, and taxing only after, was something new to our administrators.

Issue of a national currency

An estimate of the cost was prepared and the States printed the money required, which was paid to those who either worked on the project or furnished materials for it.

As the new currency was paid out into circulation among the people, exchanges were being expedited. The wage-earners went to the shopkeepers, the shopkeepers went to the producers, the producers bought enough to increase their production.

The currency was accepted everywhere on the Island. The Government took measures against inflation by decreeing that money would be withdrawn by taxes, so it does not accumulate. And, in fact, the money was retired on schedule by taxes.

But, as the increasing activity required a corresponding volume of money, other issues were brought out by the Government for other works.

On October 12. 1822, the new Market House was completed and opened. Not a penny of public debt on this public enterprise.

The bankers intervene

At the time of the original issue, there was no Bank upon the Island. This explains, without doubt, why there was no opposition to the issue of State money.

But ten years after the first issue, the Island had become so prosperous, thanks to the activity allowed by a sufficient volume of money, that the banks of England had an eye on this Island.

English bankers set up branches in the Island and brought the population around to orthodox rules. "It was unsound," they said, "to let the Government finance its enterprises without getting into debt.

The bankers did everything to stop further issues, to introduce the system of interest bearing loans to the Government, and to withdraw from the Island the State money that had been paid out into circulation.

There was some resistance, but the bankers won their point, with their usual methods; and on October 9. 1836. the States of Guernsey had abdicated their sovereign prerogative over the control of the volume of money. From then on, the amount of the national currency decreased gradually, and was replaced by money issued by private bankers in the form of loans getting the Island into debt.

Nevertheless, there is still about 40,000 Pounds Sterling ($200,000) of national currency outstanding at this date in the Island. (According to Gertrude M. Coogan in Money Creators, published in 1935)

Why a financial problem?

As we can see, with natural resources, workers, and a bit of common sense, there is no financial problem.

But when shrewd exploiters want to regulate economic activities according to their power and their profit, there the financial problem arises.

O course, minds in search of arguments to justify the present regime will say that Guernsey was only an insignificant small Island: that the control of the volume of money by the representatives of the people is good for a small country, but not for a big country.

All right. Take note of what these Gentlemen object to you to day. Next week, these same Gentlemen will tell you that the money problem cannot be solved properly in a small territory or province, but must be brought to a federal or even an international level!

It was not Social Credit yet in Guernsey from 1820 to 1836. No doubt that the development of that time and that place would not have allowed to go as far as to give a dividend to consumers. But it was already a non-debt-bearing national currency, issued in accordance with the possibilities in front of the needs.

The issues of national currencies by the "States of Guernsey" caused neither inflation nor idleness. They created activity and prosperity. But these issues did not make any slaves, and that is, why the bankers intervened.

Louis Even

THE YOUNG PEOPLE WANT A NEW FINANCIAL SYSTEM!

They want the benefit from the fruits of modern technology!

BY LOUIS-MARIE ROY

Nowadays, new technology is present more and more in industry. But too often, the replacement of man by machine brings discontent among the persons who are replaced. The introduction of a machine means the loss of jobs. Thos who are laid off say, "How will I get the products made by the machine, as I do not receive a wage?" But this reflection is due to looking at the problem from the wrong direction.

The replacement of a man by the machine in production should be an enrichment, which delivers man from worries that are purely material, and would permit him to do other activities. Let us say, for example, that I spend about thirty minutes a day washing dishes after meals. If, one day, I decide to buy a dishwasher, I would not worry about what I would do with that thirty minutes extra liberty. No, I know what I would do with my free time. If, on the contrary, the replacement of man by a machine is the cause of care and privation, it is simply because we refuse to adapt our financial system to this progress.

Why is the present financial system primitive and outdated? To explain it, I will make a simple comparison.

Imagine a primitive world without any technology, where the strength of each and every person is required to produce the goods necessary for the welfare of each person. In this world, a financial system like the present one, where the remuneration is directly related to employment, is justifiable because all the members of this society receive a wage for their work, and permits them to procure the goods they produce.

On the other hand, imagine a world (fictitious, but possible just the same) where a person would not need to work to produce the necessary goods for the welfare of one another, a world where the machine, and only the machine, is capable of furnishing goods. This world, even if it is fictitious, is very desirable. All men would be free and able to do the activity that they prefer without the worry of production. The remuneration would be distributed in ways other than in the form of salary, because man would not participate in production. The remuneration would be distributed in an equitable way in form of a dividend. This dividend would be justifiable because technology is a common heritage.

No one can deny that technology is a human heritage that belongs to each and every person, because it is the past generations that brought us this technology, which should be at the service of man, and not man at its service. It is a heritage for us, in the same way as solar energy, the formidable power of the waterways that provide us with hydroelectric dams, the power of the wind, the soil that furnishes us with an abundance of fruits and vegetables, et cetera, are.

Because we live in a world where technology and human effort unite forces in the production of goods, it is desirable that man be paid, in part, with a salary for his efforts in the process of production, and the other part with a dividend for the effort of technology and the machine.

Some will ask: "But who will pay for this dividend?" This dividend should be provided by our Governments, and not by our taxes. The Government should take back its right to create the money necessary for the smooth running of the economy; to create money instead of borrowing it with interest from private banks. Borrowing at interest only has the effect of creating an unpayable debt, because the Government must return more money than it borrowed from the banks.

The public debt in Canada has risen today to over $five-hundred billion. Yet, today, Canada is without a doubt richer in goods than it was before the arrival of the first European settlers about four-hundred years ago. After these valiant people planted the cross in the soil, they began to develop Canada. And after them, their successors for three centuries improved the agriculture, made roads, bridges, and industries. All of this lineage of workers should certainly not have left Canadians to live in the twentieth century with only a heritage of debts...

It is the primitive and dishonest financial system that we need to correct and adapt to technology. Then we could applaud the arrival of auto-

mation in our industry, instead of complaining about it.
Today's financial system is not adapted to progress.
It paralyzes the whole economic system.

Michael Journal!
From January-February 2004

Social Credit, for a healthy economy!

BY LOUIS EVEN

New readers of the "Michael' Journal may be puzzled by the ideas – which are new to them – contained in this paper regarding economics an finance, even though these ideas seem logical, and their application would bring a ray of hope into their lives. Where do these theories, which are so different from what is practiced today, com from? What is this "Social Credit"(Common Dividend), a term that is not even mentioned in current economic textbooks? Would it be a stroke of inspiration from the editors of "Michael"?

No. The "Michael" Journal certainly spreads with much fervor what is considers to be an illuminating revelation: a discovery that arrived at the right moment to settle most of the problems of economic and social nature that cause anguish to our world, whereas today's huge progress should open new brilliant horizons for our World. But the "Michael" Journal is not the author of this revelation.

C. H. Douglas

At the origin of Social Credit, there is one name, the name of a man of genius, a Scot: Clifford Hugh Douglas.

Mr. C. H. Douglas was not one of so many monetary cranks and fanatics, who belief that they know, how to reform the financial system. He was well prepared and suitable for the job as a critic and reformer. His career and development in Britain before and during World War I promoted his destination as a monetary critic.

Douglas was an engineer by trade. A brilliant engineer, who was entrusted with important projects. He was, in India, Chief Engineer and

Manager for the British Westinghouse Company; in South America, Deputy Chief Electrical Engineer for the Buenos Aires and Pacific Railway; back in England, he was employed on the construction of the London Post Office Tube Railway; then, during World War I, he was Assistant Superintendent at the Royal Aircraft Factory in Farnborough, England.

Douglas was also an expert in cost price accounting. It is for this expertise that the British Government asked him to go Farnborough in 1916 to sort out "a certain amount of muddle" in the Aircraft Factory's account.

Douglas never bore the title of economist; he would have considered this as an insult anyway because of the monument of errors, based on false premises, in economic teaching in universities. Yet, Douglass was actually the greatest economist of all times with his diagnosis of the major flaw in today's economics, and with the proposals he formulated to solve it.

A disciple of Aristotle in philosophy, Douglas considers the various functions of the economy in relation with their proper ends, and he subordinates appropriate means to these ends. He does it as an engineer, proposing ways that are both straight, simple and potentially efficient. He also does it with the absolute respect of natural and moral laws: there is, he said, an order of laws in nature, a" canon" that can not be violated. Douglas was also concerned about preserving individual freedom and responsibility, and about restoring every individual in his rights. Institutions of every nature – political, economic, social – must serve the individual, and not dominate or choke him, or hinder his freedom of choice and dictate his way of life.

These principles and concerns for the human person are the least of the worries of the present monopoly of credit and of the industrial giants created or helped by this monopoly. His principles would put financial credit at the service of skills. Gradually and quickly, massive and depersonalizing hiring could give way to free association that would take on the responsibility of supplying goods and services that answer the needs of the population. The individual would regain the freedom to accept or refuse his personal participation in every undertaking that asks for his help.

The monopoly of money and credit, and its loyal supporters, quickly saw in Douglas's proposals a threat to their privileged situation, which thy absolutely wanted to maintain, even though it was harmful to the community. They therefore made use of their powerful influence over means of communication, governments, institutions, and man in high places, to boycott the teaching of Douglas. First, it was a conspiracy of silence; then, a false representation of Douglas's theories in order to discredit them; and then, by throwing people into confusion by degrading the term "Social Credit" and by pushing ambitious people to use the term to designate a political party.

But Douglas left writings, and made disciples in several countries, including Canada, especially in French Canada; these disciples continue to diffuse his teaching. The accumulation of the bad fruits of an unsound system cannot fail to force the governments to admit, even reluctantly, many assertions of Douglas against which the whole cohort of official economist rose up. Thus, for instance, the gold standard myth has disappeared from national currencies, and the monetary function of gold has become less and less important on the international level. And what did they do with this other sacred cow, the balanced budget? The governments were forced to disregard this so-called necessity, which was taught as a matter of life or death by orthodox economists. If governments did not have recourse to unbalanced budgets, all economic life would have been killed with the present financial system.

When governments are in trouble, thy thus borrow something from Douglas's teaching, but they cook it in the sauce of the present system, just like in the case of budgets, with "KEYNES" as the cook. And because of this cooking, instead of a financial reflection of realities, the creation of public wealth is expressed by an increase in the public debt. This is why Douglas's disciples must be able to distinguish, and not take for authentic Social Credit, any social security measure being adopted to alleviate very aggravating situations.

A tranquilizer may relieve a suffering person, but it does not cure him. The present system may have recourse to all kinds of pills, but it remains sick. Social Credit would create a healthy economy, and is infinitely better.

It was during the First World War that the engineer C.H. Douglas, with the experience of several past works done in India and elsewhere, carefully examined the financial sector of the economic system, found its flaws, and worked out appropriate measures so that the economic system could fulfill its proper function. This work was completed in 1917, and the first writings of Douglas on this subject were published in 1918 in form of articles in reviews and in economic pages of newspapers; then in the book, "Economic Democracy", which was first published in 1919. Other books and pamphlets followed, accompanied by lectures in England, Australia,

Japan, Sweden, and Canada. Douglas died on the Feast of Saint Michael, on September 29.1952.

Credit

Social Credit is not a fabrication of the mind based on unreality. It is the fruit of discoveries made and analyzed by a superior mind.

Douglas was able to discover facts and defects in the workings of the present capitalistic system; flaws inherent in the bookkeeping of the price system, even if this bookkeeping was accurate, and also defects related to forgetting or perverting ends and means in economic functions. He was able to examine how these defects harmed the smooth running of the social and economic organism. He was able to draw conclusions, and than show how to rehabilitate capitalism, how to make it a wonderful servant of individuals and of the community alike, an enrichment and liberation for all, instead of looking for solutions in a Fabianist or Marxist socialism, which is tyrannical, degrading, and deceiving for the peoples that are sub-jected to it.

Let us mention some of the discoveries that led Douglas to enunciate his Social Credit proposals.

The first discovery concerns "Credit". During the completion of the works he was in charge of as an engineer, he had more than once been told to postpone work because of the lack of financial credit. These works were physically easily feasible, and the local population needed them badly, but they had to be stopped, not because of lack of manpower or materials, but because of lack of money. This was certainly not very bright. What was the trouble with money, of which the presence or absence conditions the lives of men, as though this presence or absence was due to inevitable natural phenomena?

Douglas soon discovered that virtually al the money upon which eco-nomic life depents is nothing but mere entries in bank ledgers, credited to borrowers. Not palpable money (cash), but credits that circulate through cheques, transferring sums from one account to the other. Why limit the liberation of these credits, when it is the only thing missing to make use of the productive capacity and to answer real needs?

Then, Douglas was not long to discover that the true base of any money – either coins , cash or cheques – is the productive capacity of the nation. The gold standard as the basis of money does not make any sense. When one wants to make bread, one does not dig to find some metal, but one rather cultivates a field and sows wheat.

And since the basis of financial credit, the productive capacity, is almost limitless today (at least to answer the basic needs of all), restricting financial credit to make use these possibilities of production, as long as they are not exhausted, or as long as basic human needs are not answered, is unjustifiable, odious and criminal.

A real social capital

Then considering the factors of this modern productive capacity, it is obvious that it is more and more due to the use of machines that are more and more sophisticated, and less and less due to the use of human labour. The biggest real capital of production is not money, but machinery; the progress made during the centuries, especially during the last two centuries, when the driving force, first of steam, replaced workers, horses, watermills and windmills, to drive machines. Mankind was entering the era of motorization, which has greatly expanded since that time with electric motors and internal combustion engines. We are now entering the era of automation.

But this progress, this succession of inventions, of technical improvements, could never have taken place without life in society, an ordered society, which allows the division of labour, specialization, research, the transmission of knowledge. No present human being can pretend to be, more than any other person, the owner of all these community assets which are inherited from past generations. All the members of society are coheirs of these assets, and they must all equally benefit from them.

To limit benefits only to investors and employers, who make this great common capital yield, is an injustice towards the rest of the community and coheirs.

A social dividend to all!

It is from this consideration that Douglas draws his proposal of a periodical dividend to every citizen, whether this person is employed or not in production. Because of progress, which is a common good that becomes more and more important in today's production, whereas human labour is less and less required in production, purchasing power must be more and more made up of dividends to all, and less made up of salaries linked to employment. Douglas explains: "The distribution of consumer money to individuals shall be progressively less dependent upon employment.

That is to say that the dividend shall progressively displace the wage and salary, as productive capacity increases per man-hour." The simple reason is that this increase is the fruit of progress (a common capital), and not the fruit of greater effort of the employees.

Here is something that clashes head-on with the financial regulation that states that all distribution of purchasing power must be bound to participation in production. It also goes against the call for higher wages, which are the reward for human effort, since human effort diminishes in length and intensity, because of progress.

The fact that financial credit is based on productive capacity, and that productive capacity is due in larger part to a community inheritance, suggest that the status of capitalist must be granted to every member of society, from the cradle to the grave. The practical modes of implementing this status must be adapted to the type of economy of the particular country that adopts this philosophy of distribution.

Our "Michael" Journal has often wrote on this dividend to all, and still will in the future. But let us point out this for now: Douglas studied the economic situation, drew conclusions, and looked for solutions. He did it as a realist, in a logical way, and by respecting the dignity of the human person In presenting his principles, he did not refer to what our Catholic sociologists call "the social doctrine of the Church" (Douglas himself was an Anglican, but who highly respected Catholic teachings). It is nevertheless the implementation of Douglas's Social Credit proposals that would best allow the realization of many points of the social doctrine of the Church.

One only has to think about what attention is paid today to the social function of private property: Who cares about it? Yet this function is more relevant than ever, in a world where the means of production is owned by less and less people, and only 8 people out of 20 can get an income through employment in production. Will not the social dividend to each and every individual automatically ensure them with a share in the fruits of private enterprise?

No wonder that Douglas's Social Credit lends itself better to the principles of a just and human economy, since the present economic organism is vitiated by a financial system of economic life; Douglas rejects this falsehood categorically. The agreement with facts, the truth, is more able than lies to put the economy in keeping with natural, human, and Christian principles.

The dividend is linked to no conditions, it forgets no one, it punishes no one, it harms nobody's interests. Just compare it with the governments who flounder with all kinds of tax measures to try to hide nauseating wounds without attacking the cancerous financial system that causes these wounds.

Prices!

Douglas wrote that any financial reform that ignored the price issue was doomed to failure. What would be the use of a reform that increases the revenues of the consumers, if prices also increase? This would be no more intelligent than wage increases, followed by price increases or tax increases. Purchasing power is made up of two things: money in the hand of the consumers, and prices asked by the retailers for their goods. It is the ratio between these two things that matters. With $15, you can bay only three-quarters of what is sold for $20. If the amount of money you have is doubled, you have now $30, but if the price of the same goods is doubled, they are now sold for $40. You will therefore find yourself in the same situation as before, being able to buy only three- quarters of this production. This is simple arithmetic.

The ideal thing is a ratio of one, an equality between the means of payment and the prices. This is precisely one of Douglas's proposals:

"The cash credits of the population of any country shall at any mo ment be collectively equal to the cash prices for consumable goods for sale in that country,"

Douglas adds (we will explain it later in this article): "whatever the cost price of these goods is."

Before this proposal, orthodox economists said contemptuously: "Sir, it is so, and it has always been the case; the price of any good is the sum of the money spent during its production, so the total amount of the money distributed to the consumers is always equal to the total of the prices."

Economists have kept saying that for over a century, but facts have been showing the contrary for over a century alike. These economists do not talk about facts; they only repeat what they consider to be an axiom, and the would like to submit facts to this axiom, even though the facts do not fit. Douglas, on the contrary, first considers the facts, then applies himself to finding an explanation to them, and then looks for a way to correct what can be corrected.

"A "cannot buy "A "+ "B "

In the case of purchasing power, Douglas explains that the cost incurred during production are divisible into two distinct categories: 1. Money distributed to individuals, therefore to the consumers, like wages. He calls these "A" payments; 2. payments made to other organizations for raw materials, machinery, etc.: Douglas calls these costs "B" payments. Both costs ("A" + "B") are included in the prices. The consumers receives "A" payments, but the prices are a compound of "A" +"B". It is evident that "A" cannot buy "A" + "B", unless the consumers receive the equivalent of "B" from a source other than the payments made during production.

The first objection that orthodox economists raise is that sooner or later, "B" payments become "A" payments, when the other organizations that receive the "B" pay ments distribute these payments to their own employees or shareholders. The trouble with this objection lies precisely in the words "sooner or later ", because these objectors do not take into account the time element involved. Douglas does take it into account; as an engineer, he knows that there is no equality between 100 revolutions per hour and 100 revolotions per minute, even if there are 100 revolutions in both cases.

What is called Douglas's "A" + "B" theorem has been the subject of confrontations between economists and Douglasists for years. But the amusing side of this controversy is to see the economists who refuse the explanation given by Douglas of an existing fact, and who want to draw the conclusion that this fact does not exist, instead of looking themselves for a solutions to a fact that con not be denied.

It is indeed undeniable that, despite the accuracy of cost price bookkeeping, the purchasing power of the public is not equal to the prices of the finished goods for sale. The economists themselves, while denying this disparity, advocate economic policies that confirm its existence. Are they not the first to promote exportations, and to qualify as favorable the fact of exporting more than what one imports? They certainly do not mean that a country is richer in goods when more goods go out of the country than come in, but thy say it is a "favorable balance to trade" because these exportations cause more money to enter the country, thus increasing purchasing power and filling the gap to buy domestic production.

Likewise, do they not ask foreign investors and governments to create jobs for the unemployed, in works that do not put goods for sale, like capi-

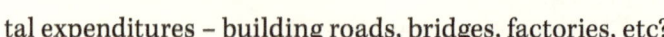

tal expenditures – building roads, bridges, factories, etc?

And does not the government get into debt for 15 or 20 years for goods that our country can make but cannot pay for, since the production of public goods does not distribute enough money to pay for them in taxes, just as the production of consumer goods does not distribute enough money to pay for them in prices?

This explains why there are so many sales on credit, and why individuals have to get into debt to be able to purchase finished goods. These debts represent money borrowed to markup for part of the "B" payments that are not yet, or no more, in the hands of the public when the finished good is put for sale on the market, when the price "A" + "B" arrives at the same time as this finished good.

What would you think of the following reasoning: "All men who are born, die, sooner or later. Thus deaths liquidate births. So the population of the world neither increases nor decreases. It is in balance!"? You would certainly replay: "Idiot, you do not take into account the rate of births and the rate of deaths, which are not the same.

Well, orthodox economists reason just like the reasoning above. They do not take into account the rate of the creation of the prices, which is not the same as the rate of the distribution of purchasing power to pay for the total cost of the finished good.

There is a price that appears in front of the consumers at the same time as a new finished good appears on the shelves of a store, but the elements of purchasing power ("A" payments and "B" payments) reach the public in different periods. Some money reaches the consumers before the finished good is put for sale, some money reaches them after, and some money never reaches them.

Correction

This disparity is inherent in the present system. How can it be corrected? Not by falsifying the cost price, which is the result of accurate bookkeeping, and which must be recovered in full by the producer if he wants to stay in business and continue to produce. The right way to correct this disparity is to increase purchasing power through another channel, which reaches the consumer directly without going through production, therefore without being included in the prices. Another way can be to lower prices to the level of the means of payments in the hands of the consumers. In both cases, the ideal purchasing power would have been reached, a ratio of one; an equality between the prices and the means of payment.

This is what is advocated by Douglas, with a combination of these two ways. With the dividend to all, based on real rights (as explained above), purchasing power is increased without going through production costs; and with a general discount on every retail price, a discount that is calculated scientifically, and which establishes a perfect ratio (an equality) between prices and means of payments. This discount would be compensated to the retailer by the "National Credit Office."

All this evidently presupposes the existence of a financial system that is flexible enough to be able to reflect the facts of production and so consumption, to allow free producers to meet the demand of free consumers.

A flexible financial system, this is what Social Credit is all about. Social Credit considers the financial system to be nothing but a matter of bookkeeping, and its function must be to serve, and not to lead the economic organization of our nation.

This is just, well-ordered, and easily feasible as well, as long one begins to admit that financial credit is based on real credit, that is to say, on the productive capacity of our country, which is basically social wealth.

The just price!

About prices. Douglas discovered a truth, of which the very revelation puts him above all economists, who only repeat what they read in their textbooks, which only reproduce what was written in previous textbooks.

Douglas expresses this truth as follows:

"The just price of production is consumption."

This means that the real cost of production is not the same as the financial cost, even though this cost price is accurate.

Considered in real terms, the real cost of a finished good is the total amount of what was consumed during the process of its manufacture. If we consider, for instance, the making of a piece of furniture. The destruction of timber, the wear and tear of tools and machinery, the food, clothing and shelter used up by those engaged in its production, are the physical cost attached to its manufacture. The totality of these physical costs, or all those goods and services consumed during the construction of this piece of furniture, constitute its real cost.

If the consumption (wood, wear and tear, food, etc.) is expressed in monetary units, then one obtains the real cost of the finished good expressed in financial terms. This cost can be quite different from the cost price. If on the one hand, the wages distributed for the making of a living room set amount to $100, this amount is totally included in the cost price. But if the employees spend only one part of this $100—let us say $60—in consumer goods, the cost price of this set will be $40 higher than its real cost. On the other hand, if an accident occurs during the making of this set and some employees are injured, their hospitalization will represent more expenditures, so the real cost of the finished set could be also higher than the cost price.

Of course it is impossible to know the real cost of every article produced, for the simple reason that a contractor only knows the expenses incurred by his enterprise, but does not check how those he pays will use this money; besides, that is non of his business, anyway. On the Other hand, one can easily know, expressed in monetary units, how much was produced in our country during one year, and how much was consumed.

Let us suppose, for example, the national accounts show that in one year the country's total production has reached a value of $40 billion, and that during that year, total consumption reached $30 billion. One can conclude that, while the country has produced $40 billion of wealth, it, at the same time caused $30 billion of wealth to disappear (through consumption or depreciation). One therefore had to consume $30 billion of wealth in order to produce $40 billion of wealth. The real cost of this production is therefore only three-quarters of its bookkeeping cost.

Moreover, the authors of this production must recover all their expenditures – $40 billion – to meet their obligations and stay in business. And yet, the population of the country must pay only for what it consumes. One cannot ask a man to pay for four loaves of bread when he consumes only three. It is the same thing for the population of the country as a whole. One cannot ask it to pay $40 billion, when it actually consumes only $30 billion of goods.

This is why Douglas says that the "just" price of production is the cost of consumption, no matter what its bookkeeping cost. In the example given above, the "National Credit Office" would decree a 25% general discount on retail prices. The buyer would pay only $3.00 of what costs the retailer $4.00. The "National Credit Office" would pay back to the retailer the $1 that was discounted.

After this period of one year, the ratio between the cost of price (bookkeeping price) and the real cost could be different, and the discount will be calculated accordingly, but always scientifically, according to statistics, to the facts of production and consumption, resulting from the free facts of free producers and free consumers.

The "National Credit Office" only records these facts; it neither creates nor dictates them. Its function is to fulfill the objective set by the law of the country concerning prices: to establish a balance between prices and purchasing power, without harming the producers. This objective (the compensated discount) would be as just and social as the other objective of the "National Credit Office—the "Periodical Dividend" to all.

Except perhaps in temporary periods like wars or natural disasters, consumption cannot be greater than production, so the just price cannot be bigger than the cost price. In a general way, the just price would be lesser than the cost price, since there would be the general discount, which is just the opposite of inflation.

As for the objection of some that some retailers would be tempted to increase their prices, seeing that people would have more purchasing power because of the dividend, it does not take into account several things: first, competition would continue to exist; second, the modes of implementation of the just price would discourage or neutralize the retailers who want to cheat, since these retailers would have either the choice to join this system that is sound for all, or to go out of business.

Besides, once money becomes a simple matter of bookkeeping to express the movement of wealth, its production and consumption, a totally different mentality will replace the mentality of the domination by money.

To have an idea of what would become of the relationship between people in the economic, social, and political life, one must consider them in a climate that got rid of the financial nonsense, of the tyranny it exercises, and of the harebrained schemes it imposes.

Louis Even.

The national debt must be written off.
For if it is paid off, the people will have been starved to
death.

Towards Social Credit by Apostolate and Tenacity!

BY LOUIS EVEN

"History teaches how the most fruitful ideas advance slowly when they clash against contrary interests. Experience has shown a hundred time that to make rational solutions known, reason alone is not sufficient. He who represents the interest of others, he who fights for them, should be dominated by the will to serve. He should believe in the righteousness of his cause, and dedicate himself without reserve to a great work" Pius XII, June 10. 1953.

The Social Creditors who are surprised to see their doctrine taking time to prevail, and the legislators of their country to be informed of it, find their answer in the first sentence of that quote mentioned above, which is a fact of history. We have as an example, the centuries of Christianity it took before slavery was abolished from all countries, even the Christian ones.

A fruitful idea, but powerful adversaries!

All the Social Creditors believe that Social Credit is a fruitful idea. How many fruits, which are impossible to obtain under the present economic-financial climate, could a civilization, blooming under the sun of Social Credit, bring! Once the constant worry for the daily bread disappears in the "unhindered" distribution of an abundant production, the people could better enjoy – at least in the measure that they would want to – activities superior to the simple economic function.

But if Social Credit is a fruitful idea, it also clashes against contrary interests, that are also powerful.

At present, the technological progress of production as a result of a common heritage, transmitted and enlarged from generation to generation, where each living person is the coheir, who should receive his part in the fruits of production, is immediately accused of being a dangerous theorist by those who have managed to put their claws on almost all resources. Relatively few but powerful, they posses efficient means to oppose you with a barrage of politicians, economists, sociologists, and even moralists.

And if, in the name of this common heritage, you claim a regular dividend for each citizen, liberating him from poverty and conditions that prevent him from organizing his own life: you are then accused of a grievous attempt against the established order – this so-called "order" by which those who control money and credit have become the masters of our lives, and who condition the right to breathe.

Those who wish to dominate and control others have no intention of recognizing the liberating measures proposed by Social Credit. How could they continue to dominate men who would not have to choose between submission and starvation?

Social Credit is definitively one of the fruitful ideas that clashes against contrary interests.

Yet the remarkable propositions of Social Credit are so logical! There application would resolve, or would at least help in resolving, a multitude of problems that are especially, and almost exclusively, of the financial kind. If everything that is physically feasible and legitimately demanded by the population was automatically made financially possible, how quickly would the things that cause the most headaches in every administration, from the family to the highest of governments, disappear! This solution should be brought to the attention of all!

No doubt! But, as the second sentence of the citation say so well: "Experience has shown a hundred times, that to make rational solutions known, reason alone is not sufficient". This is why men gifted with reason are obstinately searching elsewhere for unobtainable solutions, instead of adopting the rational solution of Social Credit.

What should we do?

So, should we give up the fight, and leave the administrators to uselessly struggle? Should we leave people to their tribulations, because they themselves are generally so unwilling to search for a solution, and the majority remains so apathetic, even after having discovered the great light of Social Credit?

No, on the contrary! It would be like taking the yeast out of the dough while still expecting it to rise. The less help you have, the harder you have to devote yourself.

The ending of the citation indicates a rule of conduct:

"He who represents the interests of others, he who fights for them, should be dominated by the will to serve. He should believe in the righteousness of his cause, and dedicate himself without reserve to a great work."

The Louis Even Institute for Social Justice has made these recommendations its own, and always wishes to inspire its members with them.

"He who represents the interests of others"—this is what a true Social Creditor, a true Pilgrim of St. Michael, should be. He does not pursue Social Credit for himself only, but for all the community, for every family, for every person in the community. It is not a paid function like that of a politician; it is a mission of dedication that he himself embraces.

"He who fights" for others—not he who pursues his own interests nor the satisfaction of his personal ambition. Even less, not he who takes advantage of the dedicated work done by others.

The real Social Creditor is then a great servant. He is an apostle who gives of himself, and not a politician who is given honors and money.

"To dedicate oneself without reserve"—this is certainly not a language for politicians; it is a language for unselfish and noble-hearted men and women who want to do their part for the good of all, by giving themselves to a work that they believe is truly great.

Conclusion

We will now end this study on a sound and effective financial system. Not because we exhausted the subject, but we believe that we have enabled the reader—or better yet, the student—to tackle, in the light of Social Credit (Common Dividend), just about all the economic problems which can come up, often with considerable social incidences.

To tackle them in the light of Social Credit (Common Dividend) means to make a clean sweep of all purely financial limitations.

There are no purely financial problems with Social Credit (Common Dividend). Neither to implement the country's productive possibilities nor to distribute adequately the fruits of production, while forgetting no one.

And this, without the need to nationalize any enterprise; without looking for an utopian way to equalize the standards of living; without revolutionizing the established methods of production and marketing; without suppressing the reward to those who, by their activities of entrepreneurs, producers or retailers, implement the means of producing and offering the wealth to the population.

We can add that a financial system reflecting reality, like Social Credit (Common Dividend), would allow a country of immense production to give some of its plenty to the countries suffering from hunger.

The abolition of the purely financial hindrances gives way to prospects of enriching developments for all, enrichments of a cultural as well as a material nature, but incompatible with the defects of the present financial system.

Supplement

The monetary system during the "Third Reich" by

RUDOLF RICKES

I hope it would be of interests for a reader of this pamphlet to know, how the monetary system was handled in Germany during the "Third Reich under Hitler"? He certainly did not go to banks or to the President of the Reichsbank, his Henchman Dr. Hjalma Schacht, to beg for interest free Money, for all his ambitious plans in rebuilding Germany's economy and later the Rearmament and Wars!

As a Dictator he didn't need that. He ordered the banks to make the Money for him, of course interest free and they obliged. Later, after the war, when everything was over, the German people had to pay in 1948 with a currency reform of 10 old Reichs Mark to 1 Deutsche Mark for the reckless undertakings of their Führer. A monetary reform according to C.H. Douglas was not by the Victorious Powers considered.

Address: The one who wants to go deeper in to the Subject, we recommend buying the Book: "The grip of Death" from "Michael Rowbotham" ISBM #1 897766 408

Pilgrims of Saint Michael "Michael Journal
1101 Principle Street Box 130
Rougemont—Quebec—CANADA
JOL- 1MO

COMMON DIVIDEND
PART II

PAPER MONEY

**The thoughts of Pastor "Sheldon Emry.
A study of modern Money, depth, slavery and destructive economics.
Billions for the Bankers, Depts for the People, the Real Story of the Money-Control over AMERICANS.**

"If the American people ever allow private banks to control the issue of their money, first by inflation and then by deflation, the banks and corporations that will grow up around them (around the banks), will deprive the people of their property until their children will weak up homeless on the continent their fathers conquered." Thomas Jefferson!

Americans, living in what is called the richest nation on earth, seems always to be short of money. Wives are working in unprecedented numbers, husbands hope for overtime hours to earn more, or take part-time jobs evenings and weekends, children look for odd jobs for spending money, the family debt climbs higher, and psychologists say one of the biggest causes of family quarrels and breakups is "arguments over money." Much of this trouble can be traced to our present "debt"—few Americans realize why our founding fathers wrote into Article I of "money system" – Too the U.S. Constitution:

Congress shall have the power to Coin Money and Regulate the Value Thereof.

They did this, as we will show, in prayerful hope it would prevent "love of money" from destroying the Republic they had founded. We shall see how subversion of Article I has brought upon us the horrors of which Jefferson had warned.

MONEY IS MAN'S ONLY "CREATION".

Economists use the term "create" when speaking of the process by which money comes into existence. Now, creation means making something that did not exist before. Lumbermen make boards from trees, workers build houses from lumber, and factories manufacture automobiles from metal, glass and other materials. But in all these they did not "create," they only changed existing materials into a more useable and, therefore, more valuable form. This is not so with money. Here, and here alone, man actually "creates" something out of nothing. A piece of paper of little value is printed so that it is worth a piece of lumber. With different figures it can buy the automobile or even the house. Its value has been "created" in the true meaning of the word.

MONEY "CREATING" PROFITABLE.

As is seen by the above, money is very cheap to make, and whoever does the "creating" of money in a nation can make tremendous profit! Builders work hard to make a profit of 5% above their cost to build a house. Auto makers sell their cars for 1% to 2% above the cost of manufacture and it is considered good business. But money "manufacturers" have no limit on their profits, since a few cents will print a $1 bill or a $10,000 bill.

That "PROFIT" is part of our ongoing story, but first let us consider another unique characteristic of the thing – money, the love of which is the "Root of all Evil."

ADEQUATE MONEY SUPPLY NEEDED.

An adequate supply of money is indispensable to a civilized society. We could forego many other things, but without money, industry would grind to a halt, farms would become only self sustaining units, surplus food would disappear, jobs requiring the work of more than one man or a family would remain undone, shipping, and large movements of goods would cease, hungry people would plunder and kill to remain alive, and all government except – family or tribe – would cease to function.

An overstatement, you say? Not at all. Money is the blood of civilized society, the means of all commercial trade except simple barter. It is the measure and the instrument by which one product is sold and another purchased.

Remove the money or even reduce the supply below that which is necessary to carry on current levels of trade, and the results are catastrophic. For an example, we need only to look at America's Depression of the early 1930's.

THE BANKERS DEPRESSION OF THE 1930'S.

In 1930 America did not lack industrial capacity, fertile-farm land, skilled and willing workers or industrious farm families. It had an extensive and highly efficient transportation system in railroads, road networks, and inland and ocean waterways. Communications between regions and localities were the best in the world, utilizing telephone, teletype, radio, and a well operated government mail system. No war had ravaged the cities or the countryside, no pestilence weakened the population, nor had famine stalked the land. The Unites States of America in 1930 lacked only one thing: an adequate supply of money to carry on trade and commerce. In the early 1930's, "Bankers," the only source of new money and credit, deliberately refused loans to industries, stores and farms.

Payments on existing loans were required however, and money rapidly disappeared from circulation. Goods were available to be purchased, jobs waiting to be done, but the lack of money brought the nation to a standstill. By this simple ploy America was put in a "depression" and the greedy "Bankers" took possession of hundreds of thousands of farms, homes, and business properties. The people were told, "times are hard," and "money is short." Not understanding the system, the were cruelly robbed of their earnings, their savings, and their property.

MONEY FOR PEACE? NO! MONEY FOR WAR? YES!

World War II ended the "depression." The same Bankers who in the early 30's had no loans for peacetime homes, food and clothing, suddenly had unlimited billions to lend for Army barracks, K-rations and uniforms! A nation that in 1934 couldn't produce food for sale, suddenly could produce bombs to send free to Germany and Japan!(More on this riddle later.)

With the sudden increase in money, people were hired, farms sold their produce, factories went to two shifts, mines re-opened, and the "The Great Depression" was over! Some politicians were blamed for it and others took credit for ending it. But the truth is, that the lack of money (caused by the Bankers) brought on the depression, and adequate money finally ended it.

The people were never told that simple truth and in this article we will Endeavour to show how these same Bankers, who control our money and credit, have used their control to plunder America and place us in bondage.

POWER TO COIN AND REGULATE MONEY!

When we can see the disastrous results of an artificially created shortage of money, we can better understand why our Founding Fathers insisted on placing the power to "create" money and the power to control it ONLY in the hands of the Federal Congress. They believed that ALL CITIZENS should share in the profits of its "creation" and therefore the national Government must be the ONLY creator of money. They further believed that ALL citizens, of whatever State or Territory, or station in life would benefit by an adequate and stable currency and therefore, the national Government must also be, by Law, the ONLY controller of the value of Money.

Since the Federal Congress was the only legislative body subject to all the citizens at the ballot box, it was, to their minds, the only safe depository of so much profit and so much power. They wrote it out in the simple, but all-inclusive: "Congress shall have the Power to Coin Money und regulate the Value Thereof."

HOW THE PEOPLE LOST CONTROL TO THE FEDERAL RESERVE.

Instead of the Constitutional method of creating our money and putting it into circulation, we now have an entirely unconstitutional system. This has resulted in almost disastrous, as we shall see. Since our money was handled both legally and illegally before 1913, we shall consider only the years following 1913, since from that year on, ALL of our money has been created and issued by an illegal method, that will eventually destroy the United States, if it is not changed. Prior to 1913, America was a prosperous, powerful, and growing nation, at peace with its neighbors and the envy of the world. But, in December of 1913, Congress, with many members away for the Christmas holidays, passed what has since been known as the FEDERAL RESERVE ACT. For the full story of how this infamous legislation was forced through our Congress, omitting the burdensome details, it simply authorized the establishment of a Federal Reserve Corporation, with a Board of Directors (The Federal Reserve Board) to run it, and the

United States was divided into 12 Federal Reserve "Districts."

This simple, but terrible law, completely removed from Congress the right to "create" money or to have any control over its "Creation," and gave that function to the Federal Reserve Corporation. This was done with appropriate fanfare and propaganda, that this would "remove money from politics" (they didn't say "and therefore from the people's control") and prevent "Boom and Bust" from hurting our citizens. The people were not told then, and most still do not know today, that the Federal Reserve Corporation is a private Corporation controlled by bankers and therefore is operated for the financial gain of the bankers over the people rather than for the good of the people. The word "Federal" was used only to deceive the population.

MORE DISASTROUS THAN PEARL HARBOR.

Since that "day of infamy," more disastrous to us than Pearl Harbor, the small group of "privileged" people who lend us "OUR" money have accrued to themselves all of the profits of printing our money'—and more!

Since 1913 they have "created" tens of billions of dollars in money and credit, which, as their own personal property, they then lend to our government and our people at interest, "The rich get richer and the poor get poorer" had become the secret policy of our National Government. An example of the process of "creation" and its conversion to people's "Debt" will aid our understanding.

THEY PRINT IT—WE BORROW IT AND PAY THEM THEIR INTEREST.

We shall start with the need for money. The Federal Government, having spent more than it has taken from its citizens in taxes, needs, for sake of illustration, $1,000,000,000. Since it does not have the money, and Congress has given away its authority to "create" it, the Government must go to the "creators" for the $1billion. But, the Federal Reserve, a private corporation, doesn't just give its money away! The Bankers are willing to deliver $1billion in money or credit to the Federal Government in exchange for the Government's agreement to pay back – with interest! So Congress authorizes the Treasury Department to print $1,000,000,000 in U.S. Bonds, which are then delivered to the Federal Reserve Bankers.

The Federal Reserve then pays the cost of printing the $1, 000,000,000, (about $1, 000) and makes the exchange. The Government then uses the money to pay its obligation. What are the results of this fantastic transaction? Well, $1 billion in Government bills are paid all right, but the Government has now indebted the people to the Bankers for $1 Billion on which the people must pay interest! Tens of thousands of such transactions have taken place since 1913 so that by the 1980's, the U.S. Government is indebted "TO THE BANKERS" for over $1,000,000,000,000, (trillion) on which the people pay over $100 billion a year in interest alone with no hope of ever paying off the principal. Supposedly our children and following generations will pay forever and forever!

AND THERE IS MORE.

You say, "This is terrible!" Yes, it is, but we have shown only part of the sordid story. Under this unholy system, those United States Bonds have now become "assets" of the Banks in the Reserve System which they then use as "reserves" to "create" more "credit" to lend. Current "fractional reserve" requirements allow them to use that $1billion in bonds to "create" as much as $15 billion in new "credit" to lend to States, Municipalities, to individuals and businesses. Added to the original $1 billion, they could have $16 billion of "created credit" out in loans paying them interest with their only cost being $1,000 for printing the original $1 billion!

AND THERE'S STILL MORE!

In addition to the vast wealth drawn to them through this almost unlimited usury, the Bankers who control the money at the top are able to approve or disapprove large loans to large and successful corporations to the extent that refusal of a loan will bring about a reduction in the price that that Corporation's stock sells for on the market. After depressing the price, the Banker's agents buy large blocks of the stock, after which the sometimes multi-million dollar loan is approved, the stock rises, and is then sold for a profit. In this manner billions of dollars are made with which to buy more stocks. This practice is so refined today that the Federal Reserve Board need only announce to the newspapers an increase or decrease in their "rediscount rate" to send stocks up and down as they wish. Using this method since 1913, the Bankers and there agents have purchased, secret or open, control of almost every large corporation in America. Using that control, they then force the corporations to borrow huge sums from their banks so that corporation earnings are siphoned off in form of interest to the banks. This leaves little as actual "profit" which can be paid as dividends and explains why stock prices are often depressed, while the banks reap billions in interest from corporate loans. In effect, the bankers get almost all of the profit, while individual stockholders are left holding the bag.

The millions of working families of America are now indebted to the few thousand Banking Families for twice the assessed value of the entire United States. And these Banking Families obtained that debt against us for the cost of paper, ink, and bookkeeping!

THE INTEREST AMOUNT IS NEVER CREATED!

The only way new money (which is not true money, but is "credit" representing a debt), goes into circulation in America is when it is borrowed from Bankers. When the State and people borrow large sums, we seem to prosper.

However, the Bankers "create only the amount of the principal of each loan, never the extra amount needed to pay the interest. Therefore, the new money never equals the new debt added. The amount needed to pay the interest on loans is not "created," and therefore does not exist.

Under this kind of a system, where new debt always exceeds the new money no matter how much or how little is borrowed, the total debt increasingly outstrips the amount of money available to pay the debt. The people can never, ever get out of debt!

An example will show the viciousness of this usury-debt system with its "built-in" shortage of money. IF $60,000 IS BORROWED, $255,931,20 MUST BE PAID BACK when a citizen goes to a Banker to borrow $60,000 to purchase a home or a farm, the Bank clerk then has the Borrower agree to pay back the loan plus interest. At 14% interest for 30 years, the Borrower must agree to pay $710.92 per month for a total of $255,932.20.

The clerk then requires the citizen to assign to the Bank the right of ownership of the property if the Borrower does not make the required payments.

The Bank clerk then gives the Borrower a $60,000 check or a $60,000 deposit slip crediting the Borrowers checking account with $60,000.

The Borrower then writes checks to the builder, subcontractor, etc., who in turn write checks. $60,000 of new "checkbook" money is thereby added to "money in circulation."

However, and this is the fatal flaw in a usury system, the only new money created and put into circulation is the amount of the loan, $60,000. The money to pay the interest is Not created, and therefore was Not added to "money in circulation."

Even so, this Borrower (and those who follow him in ownership of the property) must earn and TAKE OUT OF CIRCULATION $255,931, almost $200,000 MORE than he put IN CIRCULATION when he borrowed the original $60,000! (By the way, it is this interest which cheats all families out of nicer homes. It is not that they can't afford them; it is because the Banker's usury forces them to pay for 4 homes to get one!)

Every new loan puts the same process in operation. Each borrower adds a small sum to the total money supply when he borrows, but the payment on the loan (because of interest) then deduct a much LARGER sum from the total money supply.

There is therefore no way all debtors can pay off the money-lenders. As thy pay the principal and interest, the money in circulation disappears. All the can do is struggle against each other, borrowing more and more from the money-lenders each generation. The money-lenders (Bankers) who produce nothing of value, slowly, then more rapidly, gain a death grip on the land, buildings, and present and future earnings of the working population.

SMALL LOANS DO THE SAME THING.

If you haven't quite grasped the impact of the above, let us consider a small auto loan for 3 years at 18% interest. Step 1: Citizen borrows $5,000 and pays into circulation – dealer, factory etc- and signs a NOTE, agreeing to pay the Banker $5,900. Step 2 : Citizen pays $180 per moth of his earnings to the Banker. In 3 years he will have paid 36 x $180 = $6,480 to the Banker. Step 3: Citizen will have taken OUT of circulation $1480 more than he put IN.

Every loan of Banker "created" money (credit) causes the same thing to happen. Since this has happened millions of time from 1913 on (and it continues today), you can see why America has gone from a prosperous, debt free nation to a debt-ridden nation where practically every home, farm and business is paying usury-tribute to some Banker. The usury-tribute to the Bankers on personal, local, State and Federal debt totals more than the combined earnings of 25% of the working people. Soon it will be 50% and continue up.

THIS IS WHY BANKERS PROSPER IN GOOD TIMES OR BAD.

In the millions of transactions made each year like those above, little actual currency changes hands, nor is it necessary that it does so. 95% of all "cash" transactions in the U.S. are by cheque, so the Banker is perfectly safe in "creating" that so-called "loan" by writing the cheque or deposit slip, not against actual money, but AGAINST YOUR PROMISE TO PAY IT BACK! The cost to him is paper, ink and a few dollars in salaries and office cost for each transaction. It is "chequeing" on an enormous scale. The profits increase rapidly, year after year as shown below.

These are a few notes taken from Arizona newspapers in January, 1979.

"Valley Bank" posts 49% gain in profits. Gains of 49 percent in net income and 51 percent in operating income were posted last year by "Valley National Bank."

Those gains brought net income to $33,969.000 in the year ended Dec. 31 and operating income to $34,459.000. The year before, those totals were $22,836.000 and $22,8o7.000 respectively. Banks profit rose 21% "Arizona Bank" announced on Monday it had achieved a 21.2 percent in net income in 1978 over 1977. On the basis of operating income, excluding the 1977 sale of the Arizona Bank Building for $1,336.369, the bank said the increase was 43.9 percent.

Tostenrud said loans and deposits increased in the last Year: Deposits 18.8 percent to $1.353 billion and loans 21.9 percent to $951 million.

THE COST TO YOU? EVENTUALLY, EVERYTHING!

In 1910 the U.S. Federal debt was only $1 billion, or $12.40 per citizen. State and local debts were practically non-existing.

By 1920, after 6 years of Federal Reserve shenanigans, the Federal debt had jumped to $24 billion, or $226 per person. In 1960 the federal debt reached $284 billion, or $1,575 per citizen and State and local debts were mushrooming.

By 1981 the Federal debt passed $1 trillion and was growing exponentially as the Banker's tripled the interest rates. State and local debts are now MORE than the Federal, and with business and personal debts totaled over $6 trillion, 3 times the value of all land and buildings in America. If we signed over to the money-leaders all of America, we would still owe them 2 more Americas (plus their usury, of course!)

However, they are too cunning to take title to everything. They will instead leave you with some "illusion of ownership" so you and your children will continue to work and pay the Bankers more of your earnings on ever increasing debts. The "establishment" has captured our people with their ungodly system of usury and debt as certainly as if they had marched in with an uniformed army.

YES, IT'S POLITICAL, TOO!

Democrat, Republican, and Independent voters who have wondered why politicians always spend more tax money than they take in should now see the reason. When they begin to study our "debt-money" system, they soon realize that these politicians are not the agents of the people but are the agents of the Bankers, for whom they plan ways to place the people further in debt.

It takes only a little imagination to see that if Congress had been "creating," and spending ore issuing into circulation the necessary increase in the money supply, THERE WOULD BE NO NATIONAL DEBT, and the over $4 trillion of other debts would be practically non-existent. Since there would be no ORIGINAL cost of money except printing, and no CONTINUING cost such as interest, Federal taxes would be almost nil. Money, once in circulation, would remain their and go on serving its purpose as a medium of exchange for generation after generation and century after century, just as coins do now, with "NO" payments to the Bankers whatever!

MOUNTING DEBTS AND WARS.

But instead of peace and debt-free prosperity, we have ever-mounting debt and periodic wars. We as a people are now ruled by a system of Banker-owned Mammon that has usurped the mantle of government, disguised itself as our legitimate government, and set about to pauperize and control our people. It is now a centralized, all-powerful political apparatus whose main purposes are promoting war, spending the peoples' money, and propagandizing to perpetuate itself in power. Our two large political parties have become its servants, the various departments of government its spending agencies and the Internal Revenue its collection agency.

Unknown to the people, it operates in close cooperation with similar apparatuses in other nations, which are also disguised as "governments." Some, we are told, are friends. Some, we are told, are enemies. "Enemies" are built up through international manipulations and used to frighten the American people into going billions of dollars more into debt to the Bankers for "military preparedness," "foreign aid to stop communism," "minority rights," etc.

Citizens, deliberately confused by brainwashing propaganda, watch helplessly while our politicians give our food, goods, and money to Banker-controlled alien governments under the guise of "better relations" and "easing tensions." Our Banker-controlled government takes our finest and bravest sons and sends them into foreign wars with obsolete equipment and inadequate training, where tens of thousands are murdered, and hundreds of thousands are crippled. Other thousands are morally corrupted, addicted to drugs, and infected with venereal and other diseases, which they bring back to the United States. When the "war" is over, we have gained nothing, but we are scores of billions of dollars more in debt to the Bankers, which was the reason for the "war" in the first place.

BUT WAIT...THERE'S STILL MORE.

The profits from these debts have been used to erect a complete and almost hidden economic and political colossus over our nation. They keep telling us they are trying to do us "good," when in truth they work to bring harm and injury to our people. These would-be despots know it is easier to control and rob an ill, poorly-educated and confused people than it is a healthy and intelligent population, so they deliberately prevent real cures for diseases, they degrade our educational system, and they stir up social and racial unrest. For the same reason they favor drug use, alcohol, sexual promiscuity, abortion, pornography, and crime. Everything, which debilitates the minds and bodies of the people is secretly encouraged, as it makes the people less able to oppose them or even to understand what is being done to them.

Family, morals, love of Country, the Christian religion, all that is honorable is being swept away, while they try to build their new, subservient man. Our new "rulers" are trying to change our whole racial, social, religious, and political order, but they will not change the debt-money economic system by which they rob and rule. Our people have become tenants and "debt-slaves" to the Bankers and their agents in the land our fathers conquered. It is conquest trough the most gigantic fraud and swindle in the history of mankind.

And we remind you again: The key to their wealth and power over us is their ability to create "money" out of nothing and lent it to us at interest. If they had not been allowed to do that, they would never have gained secret control of our nation. "The rich ruled over the poor, and the borrower is servant to the lender" (Proverbs 22:7).

Let us now consider the correct method of providing the medium of exchange (money) needed by our people. History tells us of debt-free and interest-free money issued by governments. The American colonies did in the 1700's and their wealth soon rivaled England and brought restrictions from Parliament in England which led to the Revolutionary War, ending the colonial status.

Abraham Lincoln did it in 1863 to help finance the Civil War. He was later assassinated by an agent of the Rothschild Bank. No debt-free or interest-free money has been issued in America since then.

Several Arab nations issue interest-free loans to their citizens today.

The Saracen Empire fore bad interest on money for 1,000 years and its wealth outshone even Saxon Europe.

Mandarin China issued its own money, interest-free and debt-free, and historians and collectors of art today consider those centuries to be China's time of greatest wealth, culture and peace.

Germany issued debt-free and interest-free money from 1935 and on, accounting for its startling rise from the depression to a world power in five years. Germany financed its entire government and war operations from 1935 to 1945 without debt, and it took the whole Capitalist and Communist world to destroy the German power over Europe and bring Europe back under the heels of the Bankers. Such history of money does not appear in the textbooks of public (government) schools today.

Issuing money which doesn't have to be paid back in Interest leaves the money available to use in the exchange of goods and services and its only continuing cost is replacement as the paper wears out. Money is the paper ticked by which such transfers are made and should always be in sufficient quantity to transfer all possible production of the nation to ultimate consumers.

It is as ridiculous for a nation to say to its citizens, "You must consume less because we are short of money", as it would be for an Airline to say, "Our planes are flying, but we can't take you because we are short of tickets."

NO MORE BANKERS' PLUNDER.

Under the present debt-usury system, the extra burden of usury forces workers and businesses to demand more money for the work and goods to pay their ever-increasing debts and taxes. This increase in prices and wages is called "inflation." Bankers, politicians and "economists blame it on everything but the real cause, which is the usury levied on money and debt by the Bankers. This "inflation" benefits the money-lenders, since it wipes out savings of one generation so they cannot finance or help the next generation, who must then borrow from the money-lenders, and pay a large part of their life's labour to the usurer.

With an adequate supply of interest-free money, little borrowing would be required and prices would be established by people and goods, not by debts and usury.

CITIZEN CONTROL.

If the Federal Congress failed to act, or acted wrongly, in the supply of money, the citizens would use the ballot or recall petition to replace those who prevented correct action with others whom the people believe would pursue a better money policy. Since the creation of money and its issuance in sufficient quantity would be one of the few functions of Congress, the voters could decide on a candidate by his stand on money, instead of hundreds of lesser, and deliberately confusing, subjects which are presented to us today. And since money is, and would remain, a national function, local differences or local factions would not be able to sway the people from the nation's (citizens') interest. All other problems, except the nations defense, would be taken care of in the State, Country, or City government where they are best handled and most easily corrected.

An adequate national defense would be provided by the same citizen-controlled Congress, and there would be no Banker behind the scenes, bribing politicians to give $200 billions of American military equipment to other nations, disarming us, while alien nations prepare to attack and invade the United States of America.

A DEBT-FREE AMERICA.

With debt-free and interest-free money, there would be no high and confiscatory taxation, our homes would be mortgage free with no $10,000 a year payments to the Bankers, nor would they get $1,000 to $2,500 per year from every automobile on our roads. We would need no "easy payment" plans, "revolving" charge accounts, loans to pay medical or hospital bills, loans to pay taxes, loans to pay for burials, loans to pay loans, nor any thousand and one usury-bearing loans which now suck the life-blood of American families. There would be no unemployment, divorces caused by debt, destitute old people, or mounting crime, and even so-called "deprived" classes would be deprived of neither job or money to buy the necessities of life.

A debt-free America would mean Mothers would not have to work. With mother at home, juvenile delinquency would decrease rapidly. The elimination of usury and debt would be the equivalent of a 50% raise in the purchasing power of every worker. With this cancellation of all debts, the return to the people of all the property and wealth the parasitic Bankers and their quasi-legal agents have stolen by usury and fraud, and the ending of their theft of $300 Billion (or more) every year from the people, America would be prosperous and powerful beyond the wildest dreams of citizens today.

Since the expansionistic and greedy capitalistic system would have to have be abolished by adapting that previously discussed and improved monetary system, we would be at peace and not more fight world wars to satisfy that megalomania of our overstrained rulers. To break the insidious "Money-Lenders Conspiracy, also known as "The Power Elite", demands a superhuman effort by dedicated people, willing to sacrify their life (see Abraham Lincoln and J.F. Kennedy) for the cause in which they believe. The battle to be expected when the change is going to be forced on the "Conspiracy", will make the drive to abolish the "Slavery" in the 18 hundreds a child's-play.

WHY YOU HAVEN'T KNOWN.

We realize this small, and necessarily incomplete, article on money may be charged with oversimplification. Some may say that if it is that simple the people would have known about it, and it could not have happened. But this MONEY-LENDERS' CONSPIRACY is as old as Babylon, and even in America it dates back before the year 1913. Actually, 1913 may be considered the year in which their previous plans came to fruition, and the way opened for complete conquest of our people. The conspiracy is old enough in America so that its agents have been, for many years, in positions such as newspaper publishers, editors, columnists, church ministers, university presidents, professors, textbook writers, labour union leaders, movie makers, radio and TV commentators, politicians from school board members to U.S. presidents, and many others.

CONTROLLED NEWS AND INFORMATION.

These agents control the information available to our people. They manipulate public opinion, elect whom they will locally and nationally, and never expose the crooked money system. They promote school bonds, municipal bonds, expensive and detrimental farm programs, "urban renewal," foreign aid, and many other schemes which will put the people more into debt to the Bankers. Thoughtful citizens wonder why billions are spent on one program and billions on another which may duplicate it or even nullify it, such as paying some farmers not to raise crops, while at the same time building dams or canals to irrigate more farmland. Crazy or stupid? neither. The goal is more debt. Thousand of government-sponsored ways to waste money go on continually. Most make no sense, but they are never exposed for what they really are, builders of "billions for the Bankers and debts for the people."

So-called "economic experts" write syndicated columns in hundreds of newspapers, craftily designed to prevent the people from learning the simple truth about our money system. Commentators on radio and TV, preachers, educators, and politicians blame the people as wasteful, lazy, or spend-thrift, and the workers for the increase in debts and inflation of prices, when they know better that the cause is the debt-money system itself. Our people are literally drowned in charges and counter charges designed to confuse them and keep them from understanding the unconstitutional and evil money-system that is so efficiently robbing the farmers, and the businessmen of the fruits of their labours and their freedoms.

When some few Patriotic people or organizations who know the truth begin to expose them or try to stop any of their mad schemes, they are ridiculed and smeared as "right-wing extremist," "super-patriots," "ultra-rightist," "bigots," "money-cranks," "racists," even "fascists" and "anti-Semites." Any name is used which will cause them to shut up or will at least stop other people from listening to the warning they are giving. Articles and books such as the one you are reading are kept out of schools, libraries, and book stores.

Some, who are especially vocal in their exposure of the treason against our people, are harassed by government agencies as the EPA. OSHA, the IRS, and others, causing them financial loss or bankruptcy. Using the above methods, they have been completely successful in preventing most American people from learning the things you have read in this pamphlet. However, in spite of their control of information, they realize many citizens are learning the truth and they feel that the time of reconnaissance is near.

WHY HAVEN'T THEY TOLD YOU?

Why haven't they told you about this scandal—the greatest fraud in history has caused Americans and others to spill oceans of blood, pay trillions of dollars interest on fraudulent loans and burden themselves with unnecessary taxes?

Where are "they"? "They" are most of the politicians of the two old parties and elected officials. Most "educational" groups like the League of Women Voters, the Heritage Foundation and the American Civil Liberties Union (ACLU). All mainstream news services, such as the Associated Press and the United Press International. All mainstream daily newspapers, including the New York Times and the Los Angeles Times. All mainstream weekly "news" magazines, such as "Time" and "Newsweek." All of the above and more have been hiding the truth from you. President Woodrow Wilson has said, just before he died, "I have deceived and betrayed my Country." He referred to the "Federal Reserve Act" passed during his Presidency in 1913.

Let this be said enough from the wicked part of the "Conspiracy" against the people and it is suitable to spend a few thoughts about what will happen to our money system, if the "Conspiracy" has successfully overcome and eliminated?

The money as loans or credit will not anymore be created by the Banks together with interest, but by a special designated government department, interest free. The banks will than handle the money in trust for the people and all commerce, industry, business and every one else as usual for a service FEE and there is no accumulation of debt. Apart from that, everything else will play up to each other.

So far Pastor Sheldon Emry circa 1960.

COMMON DIVIDEND
PART III

TAKING BACK CONTROL OF OUR MONEY SUPPLY.

BY JOSEPH W. DUGGAN
SHARED VISION MAGAZINE – JUNE 1998 ISSUE.

This Part III script is also added to the original booklet to improve and complete that what is already declared extensively before in Part I and II. Inspire of the inevitable repetitions, it will bee of interest for the reader, to see things from a different point of view. Rudolf Rickes.

Money is the lifeblood of a technological society and it is extremely easy for a mere handful of individuals to control billions of people if they own and control the banking system. Most of us have heard of the golden rules, whereby whoever owns the gold, makes the rules. What we have forgotten is that we own the gold and are letting an elite banking group make rules which serve only their narrow self-interest at the expense of the vast majority of humanity.

What is money?

Initially, money had intrinsic value in gold and silver coins, the weight of which represented a certain value in goods and services. Later, notes were printed which were redeemable in gold and silver and, although once removed from precious metals, had intrinsic value as well. Currently, money is purely an agreed-upon medium of exchange for good and services based on faith in the ability of the issuing country to make good its financial obligations. Under this system, money has no intrinsic value, but whoever creates it and controls it can charge for the use of it. This is how the principle of charging fees for the use of money come about.

During the thousand-year, biblically-inspired ban on usury in the Middle Ages, lending institutions could only charge fees (not interest), and engage in investment of their client's money. This resulted in an unparalleled time of prosperity when massive cathedral's and the entire infrastructure of Europe were built. The sole purpose of interest is to enrich the few holders of capital at the expense of everyone else. The true producers of wealth – the artisans, trades people, inventors, workers, business people, etc – are slaves to the money masters who, with their compound interest system, create more debt than there is money in circulation to pay for. Through propaganda, we are told that the few scraps from their banquet tables served to us as interest on our savings and RRSP's justify their whole system. Nothing can be further from the truth.

Where Does Money Come From?

The average person thinks that the government prints the money supply and that banks lend the money we have deposited with them as savings. These have to be the two biggest lies ever foisted upon us. In Canada, the government currently creates only 1 – 2% of our money supply. We have in circulation about 7% of our money supply as paper notes printed by the "Bank of Canada" – not the federal government. The rest of our money supply has been created by the private banking institutions as a debt or loan.

Banks create money by making book entries, or computer entries, based on the collateral of the borrower. Basically, the real wealth of the borrower – his house, land, car, labour, etc – is pledged against the value of the loan requested. The lending institution merely creates a book entry out of thin air and, presto, the borrower has a deposit in his bank account or a cheque in his hand. For this book entry, the bank collects interest at a rate as low as 4% (in the 1960's) to as high as 28% (in the early 1980's). At one time, Canadian banks were required to maintain cash 5-7% reserves, limiting them to creating 26 times their reserves in loans. Currently, they have no limitations on the amount of money they can literally create out of thin air. This is a lot of control in the hands of individuals notorious for greed, corruption, and disregard for the interests of people, society, and the environment.

We now live in the age of usury, whereby some 99% of the increase in our money supply every year is created as debt by lending institutions and requires that interest be paid on it. However, only the loan is created by lenders, not the money to pay the interest. The money needed to pay the interest doesn't exist. The interest can only be paid out of the 1 –2% of the money supply created by the government. This is the basis of usury-charging compound interest which creates more debt than can be paid for by the money in circulation. The charging of interest on loans results in debt and the seizure of assets pledged to "secure" loans. When loans are written by lending institutions, figures are entered into a computer, the credit is then deposited into the borrower's account and the money supply has increased by that amount.

Excessive increases in the money supply as loans leads to inflation and spurts of economic growth. When loans are paid off and interest rates rise, recessions, depressions, and bankruptcies occur. These "business cycles" are very painful and extremely damaging ways to correct the underlying flaws of the fractional reserve system.

A major, fatal flaw in our money system is that whenever a loan is paid off, a corresponding portion of the money supply is destroyed. This is why our national and personal debts can never be paid off. It would eliminate our money supply. The great depression happened because the money supply was so diminished by tight money policies of the banks, that there was not enough money in circulation for people to buy and sell goods and services. This is a tremendous power to have concentrated among an elite group which meets secretly behind closed doors. The interest system can be eliminated when fees for the use of money are taken out of the principle borrowed and there is no compounding interest applied to loans. No wonder the term "usury" is so seldom used nowadays by economists; it actually describes how our economic system works, and that's the last thing the money masters want us to know.

Our Government is Controlled by Money.

It stands to reason that whoever controls the money the government spends, controls government policies and politicians. In Canada, the federal Government owns all the shares of the Bank of Canada (BoC), but has no voting power, even though the Minister of Finance has a seat on the Board of Directors. This is supposedly to separate the banking system from the excesses of uncontrolled government spending. However, the BoC is directly under the control of the Bank of International Settlements in Geneva, Switzerland, which dictates to all the member banks.

What this means is that, instead of our government deciding on monetary policies that benefit the majority of Canadians, we have an elite group of un-elected bankers meeting behind closed doors deciding on policies which affect us all in profound ways. Booms, busts, recessions, depressions, inflation, deflation, unemployment, interest rates, and currency rates are all under the control of this elite group which only acts in the interest of CAPITAL, not people or the environment. To get back control of our government we have to take back control of our money, rather then the private bankers. The federal government has the power to create our money supply as debt-free money through the Bank of Canada and did so during the Depression and World War II. These policies fueled the economic growth which lasted into the early 1970s. In fact, since 1974, the government has resumed its borrowing from the Bank of Canada such that we are paying $7 billion in unnecessary interest borrow from the private banks, money it could have had interest free.

Why was an Income Tax imposed on Canadians?

The Income Tax was imposed primarily to pay for the cost of borrowing money from private banks. This goes back to July 6. 1913, when the Government of Canada inexplicably enacted a law known as "An Act Representing Banks and Banking," which was cited as "The Bank Act." Under the terms of the Bank Act of 1913, exclusive jurisdiction for the control and issue of the nation's currency and credit was given away to the "Canadian Bankers Association." The consequences of this illegal transfer of power were shortly after being felt throughout the country. For example, in 1913, Canada's national debt was a minuscule $550 million. By 1917 – only four years later – it had nearly quadrupled to just over $2 billion. Today, it is roughly $600 billion.

It soon became very obvious that the issue and control of currency and credit, now out of government control, would incur a heavy debt load. However, instead of recovering those rights given away in 1913, the Federal Government decided in 1917 to put a system into place to collect "Income Taxes" in order to pay the debt and interest costs incurred by the war. This system is the "Income War Tax Act" which came into being as the inevitable result of this "Mistake," illegal as it was, that was made in 1913. Believe it or not, we are still paying income taxes under the "Income War Tax Act" which was never rescinded. Although voluntary, the origin and validity of this income tax have been distorted so that payment of the tax is now perceived as obligatory, and has become a modern form of economic "Slavery."

Shared Vision Magazine – June 1998 issue.

The greatest swindle of all Times

Society is robbed of its wealth.

The country's debt grows as it produces.

BY LOUIS EVEN.
MICHAEL JOURNAL NO. 335

Servicing the public debt

Each year, governments draw up their annual budgets. It is a program of the revenues and expenditures anticipated for the next twelve months. Whether such a budget is forecasted for the federal, provincial, or municipal governments, or for school boards, there is invariably an item listed as, *servicing the debt.*

Obviously there are expenditures: expenditures foreseen for different services and for administration; for the construction of bridges, canals, roads, public buildings; for social security, old-age pensions, family allowances, pensions for the disabled; in municipalities, for garbage disposal, street maintenance, the fire and the police departments; for the school boards, for the building and maintenance of schools, for the salaries of teachers, etc.

All of these various items of expenditure—all save one—are carefully examined by the representatives of the people in these various public bodies. Questions are asked, answers are supplied, and sometimes amendments are made before such items are approved.

All save one. Which one? The first mentioned: servicing the debt, the interest charges on the public debt. This one item is sacrosanct; untouchable; beyond any question, privileged. There is no question posed about it;

no discussion.

Funds requested for charity can be crossed out. Aid to the needy can be set a side.

Children and families can be left to go in want. Urgent public needs can be waived and neglected. But the debt, servicing the debt, the annual interest charges which have to be paid on this debt – even if servicing the debt requires a quarter, a half, three-quarters of the budget; even if taxes have to be raised to such an extent that the citizens are despoiled of their wealth, of their property – there can be no argument, no obstacle placed in the way of this item, that of serving the public debt!

To whom, then, is it so important to pay this sums, this so privileged part of the budget? Will they be turned over to people who are on the verge of starvation, and will surely perish if aid is not speedily forthcoming? Not at all. They go to Financiers. And normally one does not find these gentleman living in slums, lying on beds of straw, nor seated before empty plates.

The people robbed

But how does it happen that so many and such heavy debts lie upon the shoulders of our public bodies? Whence come these debts which the entire population must service through the payment of taxes, direct or indirect; taxes which cut heavily into the citizen's purchasing power, even when, very often, he has scarcely enough, or not enough, to meet his most essential needs?

Whey these debts? Because we accept, with almost mystical faith, to submit to a financial system which in fact constitutes the greatest swindle ever perpetrated upon mankind; a swindle which robs the people in the very measure that people produce real wealth.

To demonstrate this, it is only necessary to compare the situation of Canada today with the Canada of 50 or 100 years ago – the Canada of the pioneers.

Farms, factories, roads, schools, hospitals, and all such like, did not exist when the first colonists came to settle in Canada. All of these things have come into existents since their arrival. Progressive enrichment. Such wealth is immeasurably greater than it was 100 or 50 years ago. And yet compare the debt, the sum of all the public debts of Canada today, with the sum of the public debts in those days. Real wealth equals' financial debt – that seems to be the equation. And who goes into debt? The people, since it is the people who make the payments necessary to service the debt.

And yet it was the people of the country who, throughout all these years, have produced and piled up the vast, real wealth of Canada.

Who built the schools, the water supply system, the roads, and other public utilities? Engineers and workers. Why were these engineers and labourers able to devote themselves to the production of such wealth rather than to the production of goods for themselves personally – Because other workers in the land were producing the food, the clothes, the shoes, and the multitude of other items and services which the builders of these public goods needed for themselves personally.

In sum, then it is the people, the people all together, who by the work they have accomplished in exploiting the resources of the country – resources placed there by God for their use – the work they have done together, all across the land, which has provided, and continues to provide, the wealth of all these developments.

And yet, when the school has been finished, or the water system, or the road, or any other bit of public production, it is immediately set down as a cost in the public debt to be paid by the people. And worse – the people are expected to pay this cost, this debt, not once, but once and a half over, twice over, and sometimes more, according to the time set down for the completion of payments.

The producers are billed

Here, then, is a very curious kind of accounting – double curious – in that the bill for products is sent to the producers of these products, and not for the total of the cost of production, but far more!

To be quite logical, it is not the producers who should have to pay the cost of production, but the consumers; and they must pay for what they consume, but not more.

If I buy a loaf of bread, I pay for it because I am going to consume it. I certainly will not have to pay twice the price, for the simple fact that I am not consume it twice. And what is more certain is that the baker is not the one who is going to pay for my bread. The payer is not the producer, but the consumer, who is going to cause this particular bit of wealth to disappear.

And such should be the case with public production, the production of wealth, of goods, by the people in its entirety.

The school, the water system, the road – these things which the population has produced, are, it is true, going to be used by the people themselves. So it happens that the people who have been the producers of this wealth now become the consumers of these same goods. The population "consumes" its own public production. In the case of durable goods, this consumption takes place by degrees, as these goods are worn; it is called *depreciation.*

Very well, then, let's bill the people for what they consume, but not what they produce. Don't put the people in debt for producing a school, a water system, a road, but rather charge them for the gradual depreciation of a school, a water system, a road. This would be more in conformity with reality.

And a building can no more be "consumed" twice than can a loaf of bread. It cannot be depreciated for more than its value.

A concrete example

Some time ago, the mayor of a city in Quebec told us that the people of his town had already paid for their water system by three and a half time its cost, mainly through annual interest payments, and perhaps through writing off a part of the capital. Nevertheless, there still remained payment to be made on this water system.

So here we have a water system which has been paid for three and a half times over and yet it has not been "consumed", even once, since it is still there!

This is a perfect example of the greatest gigantic swindle which has made, and is making, the people pay over and over again for that which the people themselves produce.

And nothing is explained by saying that in the case of the people of that city and their water system, the people did not produce this system through their own labours exclusively; that materials had to be brought in and machinery used which was manufactured elsewhere. That is true. But the situation being the same everywhere, the system of finance – and of public debt – being the same likewise, it is the entire population of the country which is held collectively in debt for its collective production, one kind here, another there, even if it is at different level of governments that the people are charged with the debt and at which they must pay.

Extortion all along the way

Is it not strange that the people should submit to extortion on such a grant scale?

And so far we have spoken only of public production. Since it is the same financial system which, directly or indirectly, finances private production, setting forth its own conditions, industrialists and businessmen are obliged to pay interest for the right to produce those goods necessary to meet the needs of the country. And there again, it is definitely the people who put up the money which is demanded by this system of extortion. In public production, the money is raised through taxation. In the case of private production, the levy is made through the price.

And the consequence is that we cannot profit, or profit only in a very small way, from the tremendous fruits of progress. We are obliged to bend down under an ever growing weight of taxes, while the immense productive capacity of modern production should, in effect, make it possible for public needs to be satisfied without in any way forcing private needs to go unfulfilled. We lament the ever-increasing prices of goods and services, when, in fact, the extraordinary facility with which production can be accomplished should result in ever decreasing cost prices.

And all of this has come about because our financial system is a master instead of a servant, and as such its robs the people of the fruits of their labour, the real wealth of the country.

The origin of this swindle

But from where did this giant swindle take its origin? – It took its origin in that first act of theft, in the appropriation of the credit of society by those who make and destroy the means of payment, by those who control the gates of financial credit.

This publication has many times explained, in diverse ways, of what modern money consist, how it is created and where, what conditions are placed upon it, how it remains in existence and how it is destroyed.

Let as merely recall here that money, no matter what form it takes, does not derive its value from the material of which it is made – gold, silver, nickel, aluminum, bronze, paper, or figures set down in a ledger. "NO". It draws its value from the goods and services which correspond to it. Without goods and products, either actual or potential, all the money in the country, even if it were piled up as high as the peaks of the Rockies, would be worthless.

Goods and services are provided by the people themselves who exploit their resources, using their intelligence, their arms and hands, machines, inventions, und all the techniques of a highly developed society. All of these factors make up real wealth, real capital. It is this production capacity which gives birth to confidence in being able to live off a country. It is this country's *"REAL CREDIT"* (credit:= confidence).

And it is above all a social credit which goes far beyond the sum of the individual capacities of individual citizens considered individually. Total production would have been immeasurably smaller, even if each individual put forth even greater efforts, were it not for the fact that life in a society made it possible to conserve, add to, and pass on from one generation to another, the heritage of knowledge and skills acquired during the course of generations; and also for the fact that life in society has made possible the division of labor and the various activities that supply the community market.

But if this great production capacity is to be mobilized and set at the service of the community's needs, it is necessary that we have that thing which we call "MONEY", or as it is more commonly called today, "FINANCIAL CREDIT".

The only value financial credit has, comes from real credit. It is, in essence, nothing more than the monetary expression, the expression in figures, of real credit.

Hence it, too, is as good which is common to the community, and not the property of those who monetize real credit, or set it down in terms of figures which exercise the same function as money.

Now, this operation takes place in the banking system.

It is too generally assumed that banks are establishments set up to receive savings, and to lend out these savings in order to make a profit. The truth is quite different. What the banks lend, what they give to the borrower, is not the savings brought in by the depositors. What they lend – and the bankers know this very well – is financial credit which the banker himself creates with his pen by inscribing the amount of the loan to the credit of the borrower.

And since this financial credit, this new money loaned by the banker, is based upon the real credit of society, it is society itself which, through the intermediary of the banks, lends this new credit to the borrower. However, the banker treats this new credit as if it were strictly and solely the property of the bank. He lends it out, charging a rate of interest which must be paid to the bank, along with the original loan. The borrower must try and extract this additional money, the interest, from the public through his prices. So it is that society, the true owner of this credit, must pay for the permission to realize wealth, which in fact belongs to society.

And since this credit is essentially a social good, even though it is thus lent through the intermediary of the bank, it should be the people who derive benefit and profit from it, instead of having to be charged for it. We admit that the banks are rightly entitled to a just remuneration for their accounting work. But the amount of accounting relative to, let us say, a school, cannot be worth the cost of the school, not to say two or three times the real cost of the school.

And to carry our analysis a little further, if we consider this whole matter in terms of reality, of facts, setting aside all the vocabulary of financial terminology, any production, in the final analysis, really costs what it was necessary to consume in order to produce it. Everything that has been consumed by everyone everywhere, in one year, constitutes the real cost of all production of every sort during that year.

If our financial system were to reflect, faithfully, this set of facts, there could not be a collective debt such as we have now, for we could not, globally, consume more than we could globally, produce. Instead we would have the expression of a financial surplus, which would be the expression of a surplus of total production over total consumption.

But the financial system gives no such an expression of facts because it is false and fraudulent.

Turning their back on the light

It is 87 years since the full details of this vast swindle were exposed and explained by a genius, the Scottish engineer, "C. H. Douglas". He also demonstrated how this system of robbery and extortion and tyranny could be turned into a system of service: into a system which would put financial credit at the service of producers so that they might produce, and put adequate purchasing power in the hands of the consumers so that they might procure these products. This was to be done through the application of those principles which have com to be known as "Common Dividend" or its equivalent "Social Credit. (Note: *principles, not parties.)*

Public debts would then be changed into public assets. Instead of taxes, which deprive people of goods when there is an abundance of goods offered for consumption, there would be a dividend for each individual, which would obviate the possibility of anyone having to live in dire poverty. There would be true social security, without humiliating inquisitions, without taxation, based upon the great productive capacity of the country.

These ideas and principles, first set before the world by Douglas, have been propagated far and wide in Canada for the last 70 years by different methods, especially through the two papers of our Movement, Michael and Vers Demain. and yet one still finds men in public positions who are quite ignorant of this grand swindle, or who close their eyes to it.

The extreme and wrongly guided Socialist, for example, take after private enterprise and blame it for our economic woes. And yet private enterprise, with a social conscience, has done a fine job of producing vast quantities of all goods and services. They should rather take the big stick to financial system, which has been responsible for the astronomical debt under which the countries groans.

Unions take after the employers who pay them, instead attacking that system which lays down such financial conditions that business-men are obliged to set prices which the workers salaries can never hope to overtake.

The Separatists of Quebec attack the English Canadians and Confederation, when in fact, all the provinces are forced to submit to this same debt-engendering system, to the same system of financial tribute, to the same grand swindle.

This financial dictatorship has corrupted our whole economic life. It has given rise to an economy of wolfs. It has perverted the true ends of all economic activity by making these ends the pursuit of money. It has given rise to the universal scourge which we will call the cult of money. It is something, in essence, that is truly diabolical.

It is sheer nonsense to speak about bringing an end to such a force, to such a heresy through election fights. In fact, it cannot be vanquished by any method or any force which is purely human. One must try to replace the cult of money with the cult of service, division by unity, egoism by self-dedication.

Today, the men and women formed by our publications and our Movement, the Pilgrims of Saint Michael, are seeking to do just this. Day after day the go among the people, carrying this message of Social Credit, inviting individuals to shoulder their responsibilities, and to work togeth-er to a common end, which is the welfare of all with freedom for all.

Louis Even

APPENDIX

A CRITICAL REFLECTION

I have long considered the idea of recording my observations and critical conclusions concerning the jumble of information's whit which we are bombarded by the press, radio and television on a daily basis as long as I still have time.

The purpose of this continuous rain of more or less important news to which we are subjected, whether we want it or not, is clear to me, as it is to the majority of reasonable intelligent human beings. It is not simply the noble impulse of the bosses, and those pulling the strings, to keep us abreast of the latest events, but rather to influence our opinion and shape it to their purposes. It is the same urge that well known dictators of all persuasions used and still use it to day, to bent their dear subjects to their will. Following is a typical example of what is going on:

News media controlled

John Swanton, former Chief of Staff for the New York Times – 1953 toasting the inadequacy of his profession before the New York Press Club:

"...if I allowed my honest opinions to appear in one issue of my paper, before twenty-four hours my occupation would be gone. The business of journalists is to destroy the truth; to lie outright; to pervert; to vilify; to fawn at the feet of mammon, and to sell his country and his race for his daily bread.

"You know it and I know it, and what folly is this toasting an independent press? We are the tools and vassals of rich men behind the scenes. We are the jumping jacks, and they pull the strings and we dance. Our talents, our possibilities and our lives are all the property of other men. We are intellectual prostitutes."

The following quotation of David Rockefeller, then Chairman of Chase Manhattan Bank, speaking at the June 1991 Bilderberg meeting in Baden-Baden, Germany, is illustrative of this media control:

"We are grateful to the Washington Post, the New York Times, Times Magazine and other great publications whose directors have attended our meetings and respected their promises of discretion for almost forty years" He went on to explain: "It would have been impossible for us to develop our plan for the world if we had been subjected to the lights of publicity during those years. But, the world is more sophisticated and prepared to march toward a world government. The supra-national sovereignty of an intellectual elite and world bankers is surely preferably to the national auto determination practiced in past centuries."

(The before mentioned name "Bilderberg" distinguishes a club of a secret society of the richest and most influential people, conspiring to achieve a world government.)

Those statements speak for themselves and require no interpretation or explanation. I do not believe they reveal anything knew, but the outspokenness is remarkable. We now know how we are directed and managed, and throughout the millennia it has always been so in the development of mankind and has been the cause for all the wars and revolutions we were obliged to go through.

Virtue and vice have always fought for predominance and always will. The circumstances and the tools change, but otherwise, everything remains the same – from birth, human nature is predestined to do so.

That is a fundamental truth which was already debated by Chinese wise men and ancient philosophers thousands of years B.C. Whoever is able to reach for the book by "Lao Tse", one of the earliest Chinese thinkers and philosophers, born around 604 B.C., will be touched by the spirit of this man. Namely by the timeless spirit that once developed in him. It is not a matter of understanding all the hidden nuances and trains of thought, but simply of getting the feeling for that strange spiritual urge to seek the ultimate truth.

Even than, in the battle for political power they differentiated between the divine, good, lucid and warm "YANG" and the earthly, dark, cold and evil "YIN". They believe that Yin and Yang are active in every human being.

But let us return to virtues and vices, i. e. yin and yang. The libraries of the world are bursting with books on this subject if, as it must be, we include religious literature. So it would be superfluous to write about it again. However, it must be mentioned that from time immemorial, religion has played an important role in people's lives. Their purpose was to explain the incomprehensibility of the world in which they lived and to show the right goal in life – as seen by their founders, of course.

Amongst the mass of existing organic life-forms in this world, the first humans were social creatures, like many others, and like them were subjected to the survival instinct.

It is not the purpose of this essay to expand on that subject. My book "Social Justice Yesterday, Today, Tomorrow" addresses all that in detail, and I recommend reading it. May aim is to show that from the time the necessary orders were established among the first groups, the strongest, the brightest and, above all, the most wily held the leadership and understood how to use fraud and falsehood to retain the role for himself and his descendants or for likeminded groups. With their absolute power, they were called Kings and they established a hereditary monarchy. Contrary to the people the ruled over, they held all authority over life and death, peace or war.

That would change, however. In ancient times Greece, as it is known today, was a collection of small city-states with various independent social orders. Each had it's own army. Those city-states, which were at their peak around 450 B.C., had a political order with a constitution as their form of power and which set out the political direction. This was essentially put into practice according to the earlier methods used by the tribes whereby each member was allowed his individual vote. The Greeks called this "democracy", which originates from the word "demos" (people) and "kratos" (rule), i.e. rule by the people. Roughly speaking, this placed limits on the arbitrariness of rulers.

Regrettably, theGreek democracies were not lasting very long. The envy and resentment of their barbarian neighbors were able to conquer them and restore the old system. A period of twothausand years passed between the fall of the democratic city-states in Greece and the establishment of today's constitutional democratic forms of government. Even in a well functioning democracy of today it would be a mistake, to deny that it is possible for crafty agitators to misuse a position of power to the detriment of the people. In order to prevent this from happening, all the members of the populace would be well-advised to be extremely vigilant.

However, there is a huge difference between the noble and progressive theories of democracy as they are thought in schools and which the populace believes and reality.

Even the proposition in the American constitution – that power is exercised by the people for the people – are merely empty words. Nothing is further from this principle than the democracy currently exercised in the USA. Whoever believes that the individuals who, from time immemorial, have ruled and exploited the people through their craftiness and eloquence have now struck their colours and are content and satisfied with this fate, are under a dangerous illusion.

They have already succeeded in undermining the generally understood and generally believed principles of true democracy and exploited them for their power-hungry purposes. As in ancient times it is evident, that a small non-producing class in power, leads a lucrative life at the expense of the producing masses. But this is not all. In order to utilize the will of the people for their own purposes, the press, television and radio are being manipulated as described above. The individual personalities, although the appear in the visual field of propaganda, are merely figureheads and willing servants of the power elite. All the decisive positions in the formation of public opinion are occupied by these people and no one dares to show any opposition. In addition to that, in most cases they are multimillionaires; and who, amongst the simple voters, or group of voters, has the wherewithal to fight for a new or better concept of politic in the country? In election campaigns there is shameless lying, deceit and fear mongering – whatever the power elite deems most suitable to achieve its goal, namely to maintain absolute power over the people.

Capitalism Versus Socialism

Capitalism is an economic order in which production is determined by the interest in monetary gain (Profit) and in which people, who own capital assets determine the type, direction and extent of production.

Socialism is a concept in which the community, not the individual, is the measure of all things. From socialism, muddle heads and radical socialists developed communism, (Karl Marx) which terrified the entire western world when, after the First Welt War, Lenin led a bloody and successful revolution and founded the Union of Socialist states of Russia, the USSR. Naturally capitalism is incompatible with communism and they are mortal enemies. After long years of Stalinist rule in the USSR and the Cold War with capitalist America, the cool-headed new president,

Michael Gorbachev, was able to defuse the Communist danger whitout bloodshed.

The fall of communism in the USSR led to the decline of communism parties in western democracies and throughout the world. Besides liberal and conservative parties, only socialism and capitalism remain as adversaries in the battle for power in the nations.

Whey "Socialism" Today?

Today the word "socialism" and its associated concept are so reviled that it is risky to write about it and to interest the reading public in it. But for over a century it was used in political literature before being reduce to a degrading catchword and looked down upon. This not least because, as already mentioned, muddle heads and criminal agitators utilized it out of hunger for power over their Peoples.

Mind you, I am not in favor of the "Socialism" used for decades in class warfare and quite correctly condemned. What I mean under the term "socialism" are the ethical and noble characteristics as understood by the uneducated common man.

I would like my concept of "socialism" to be understood as born from the biblical words "Love thy neighbour and do good unto those who hate you". And it is a firm principle of mine that any actions by socialists must assure that no one is interfered with in any way and form, except in the case of visible and convinced criminal conduct. Respect and recognition of human rights must be the ruling principle.

As whit all things,"socialists" had to learn from bad experiences, but despite setbacks, they steadfastly remained convinced of the superior and noble characteristics of "socialism".

Today the dogmatic "socialism" of class-warfare as proclaimed by Marx and Engels, centuries ago, and whose political dogma its adherents attempted to impose on their people, is obsolete. It is almost unnecessary to mention, that the concept of socialism is entirely based on the concept of democracy and that the complement one another.

Today we have come so far that when someone exposes a deplorable state of affairs and publicly denounces the bad social conduct of the perpetrators and attempts to put a stop to it, he is branded as a "socialist" and silenced.

The concept of democracy developed over centuries, slowly grew amongst the most varied peoples – admittedly sometimes by force – and so, in the same way, must the concept of socialism grow from within the nations. Morals cannot be imposed through laws, so likewise it would be wrong, to impose democratic and socialistic concepts on other peoples. One can at most offer assistance, but without deliberate blackmail and only, if one's one house is in order.

It must be pointed out, that achieving the goal of a democratic and socially focused national community, all depends on politicians, having a cosmopolitan and unbigoted upbringing and education. What is important is the early recognition of crafty, power—obsessed individuals and, by exercising one's right to vote, preventing them from pursuing their desires. For democracies and socialists, vigilance is paramount in order to nip all these aberrations in the bud.

Capitalism Today

The concept of capitalism is the continuation of human development, when it was important for every living creatures, to think for himself first and so ensure his own survival, and this is what is capitalism about to day. The increase in the number of members of a tribe or a nation, necessarily brought with it social problems whose effects were limited, however, since as mentioned before, the will of the strongest dominated the tribe or the people. Today it is characterized by an unending craving for material advantages that is fueled by the media on a daily basis. The result is a striving for growth, without recognizing that growth for growth's sake is like a cancer tumor comprised only of the uncontrolled growth of body cells. This craving is most often demonstrated in the American media through their continuous advertisement that, firstly, ridiculously exaggerated and, secondly, quite obviously insult the intelligence of the people.

The same is with the very often mentioned and repeated Slogan: "He is looking for the American Dream". It is nothing else as an invitation to selfishness and greed.

It is not my intention to describe in detail the differences between capitalism and socialism—that, I assume, is general knowledge. I simply wish to point out, based on my knowledge of both, that a virtually ideal society is possibly if both adversaries are equally represented und fully respect one another. Capitalism as the engine and socialism as the break in a well function society. As unlikely as such a development seems possibly in the near future, it is nevertheless important to mobilize the intellectual forces in both camps in order to achieve this goal.

Several times already I have brought up the subject of the deplorable state of affairs in the societies of nations with respect to power and financial circumstances and I would advise the reader going back to previous articles here.

World Government Utopia or Reality? Aim of the Financiers?

BY RUDOLF RICKES

Overview of subject-matter for a "world government".

This overview is an attempt to briefly describe for the interested reader the world government desired by many, with the option of implementing it or rejecting it as an utopia. In common with many others, the author of these pages believes that Western Culture is declining and that this is, therefore, a good time to radically change the old system of states. Not that all may readers will agree with me, but I have at least dared an attempt.

Introduction.

To those who had the opportunity to read the book "The Outline of History" by H.G. Wells will be amazed how early and how often the rulers and sovereigns of large kingdoms strove to realize the idea of a single world government for all the people (in the respectively known world.)

And it were not only the rulers, but also the religions, who strove for this in order to increase the numbers of their beliefers and to spread the blessings, primarily Christianity, Judaism and Mohammedanism. The extent to which other great religions such as Buddhism and Hinduism in Asia or religions in China attempted the same, is unknown to the author.

However, in spite of all these endeavors, it was not the aim of the respective rulers and advocates of a "World Government" for all countries, to free the individual citizens from there misery and offer them an easier, more beneficial and peaceful existens, but rather only to acquire more power and wealth without any competition.

This desire weaves its way through human history like a red thread, sometimes as a heazy dream, sometimes as a pampered beautiful illusion of those with power over their people during the centuries before Christ and after right up to the present day. It is well known that even the political line of "Communism, with its slogan: "Workers of the World Unite", was involved and trough revolutions intended to enforce the power of the proletariat so thy, too, could enjouy the anticipated wealth.

Recently, her and there in the media – newspapers and television – there have been indications of how a world with a "World Government" and benefits for everyone, could be a paradise on earth. Today, this basic human desire is reinforced by the political unrest caused by the war in Iraq and between the Jews and Palestinians as well as the expectations of more terrorist attacks around the world. Everywhere upheavals, demonstrations and violent protests.

The two world wars have given frish impetus to the idea and the hope of freedom from such conflicts in the nations of the world. Therefore, in 1919, the "Leage of Nations" was created, based on the 14 Points of the American Preseident Wislson which led to an armistic to end the terrible war and to the hypocretical aim of guaranteeing peace forever, However, it became an assembly of quarrels through the fault of the victor nations and was rather weak and useless. After World War II, the victorios nations established in 1946 "The United Nations" with the same aims as in 1919. To protect the world from new convulsions caused by wars and unrest and to contribute to understanding amongst nations for the benefit of the whole world. Negotiations and communications instead of violence was and is still the motto of the so colled "United Nations" in spite of wars in Korea, Vietnam, Balkan, Afghanistan and in Iraq, not to mention a few engagements in the past.

Then there is the "Bilderberg Club", a secret society of the wealthiest and most influential people in most of the countries of the western world, devoted to achieving a "World Government". The majority of the media is owned by this world elite and here and there, in newspapers oder on television, it showers the population with its intention, without mentioning the Bilderberger's meetings and their existence.

Some articles on this subject even go so far as to demand, that any form of state power must be rejected (to make people happy). They say that no one may be forced and no one be subjected to any form of regulations made by another person without his or her consent, unless he/she is a slave. However, such a completely free society of that sort, would be short lived, because envious neighboring states or criminal elements within the state would destroy and entslave it.

Before addressing in more detail the plan to create a "World Government", we must look at what form this world government should take and who should exercise power? That it must be a form of democracy goes without saying. Whether it includes the entire Globe or only the highly developed Western countries will be a matter for an intensive debate.

An endorsment of the idea of a society without the institutions of a normal state, which satisfies the before mentioned principles of independence and freedom of each individual citizen, must be rejected, because that would lead to "Anarchy".

Text books generally differentiate between three institutions of governmental power or authority, the legislative,executive and judicial powers. However, over the centuries, a fourth power has developed, namely the "Financial Power". This power, which governs all other powers and possesses no authority from a constitution and is not subjected to any government i.e is not elected by the people, is the "Financial Power."

It is not the money that everyone has in his wallet. It is not the money invested in shares and bonds or in bank saving accounts. Nor is the financial power what governments call – inflation, – the continuous increase in prices. No, those are all small fry compared with the status and the power of the superpower being denounced here and which believes, that it is the only power capable of governing the masses – with or without democracy.

This "Financial Power" is therefore reprehensible because it exercising authority with its decision to loan money which it does not have but which it creates out of nothing as a figure in it books, in return for "INTEREST", the amount and term of which it deternines, for everyone who needs money like Governments – central or provincial, – communities, towns, businesses, corporations and for every privat citizen who needs money, like a mortgage for instance and so on. With this, it regulats the life blood of the entire national economy of every nation.

So, who in the "Financial Power" actually makes the decisions? In addition to the Bilderberger Club, already mentioned, it is kontrolled by the "IMF" (Internationaler Moneytary Fund), the world bank in "Bern," Switzerland, the UN and alle European central banks. Every well known

European member of government has at one time or another attended a Bilderberger conference and even the Seccretary General of the NATO is a "Bilderberger". This shows that the Club is intensively involved in politics.

There is another important but not well known group of powerful and influential people called "The Commission of 3000" who are also striving for world supremacy. Then there are the international or global corporations, who all crave for global market dominations.

It has already been mentioned, that the world power aspired, must have a true democratic form of government, supported by all citizen of a nation, so as to guarantee a free and peaceful life vor all.

My book "Social Justice, Yesterday, Today, Tomorrow" discusses in detail the principles of a Democracy and its originate in Greece around 450 B.C. under the rule of the statesman "Pericles". The democratic form of government is one of many, but it is the one that stood the test of time throughout history and must be the preferred form. However, not a "Money Bag Democracy" as practiced in the U.S.A. One has to be a Millionair in order to have any chance in an election campaign.

Above all, and this is not merely a suggestion but rather a condition to establish a "World Government". As already mentioned, the ideas and principles of democracy must be understood, respected, desired and demanded from the grass roots of the ordinary citizens. As with everything which has to do with the four state powers and their agencies, without which there can be no government, it must be initiated and chosen not from above by the existing powers, but from below by the ordinairy citizens,

If it is not possible in that form, then the attempt to create a "World Government" for all people must be deemed to have failed. Anything else or merely similar, is not acceptable.

In a "World Government", established on the above principles, "Social Justice" must prevail and all laws and decisions made by the Authorities and their Agencies have to reflect that aspect.

Any other form of a "World Government", as the Financiers and the todays Power Elite have in mind, must be prevented by all means.

And it also very important in order to achieve this, that all medias – Newspapers, Televisions and Radios educate the masses with the slogan "Social Justice" and:

He who has freedom and rights, also has above all, Obligations.

However, the guaranteed freedoms of each individual in this "World Government" must not serve to encourage"Anarchy", where everyone may do as he pleases. In fact,the question of how the "World Government" should be composed, has not yet been addressed. It must be a voluntary union of states, based on the will of democratic minded peoples, similar to the "Eurpean Union", the difference being, that all the member states give up their sovereignty but not their currency, which remains under the authority of its respective government.

All the member states in the "World Government" retain their four branches of powers as already explained: the "Financial Power", which must be newly included, being responsible for controlling the flow of money, the life blood of the economy. It meets the demand of capital in the state, for instance of of the government, provinces, municipalities, the economy in general and private individuals for mortgages, etc. by granting "Interestfree" loans through the banks for a one-time fee.

The benefits for all the citizen of such a "World Government" are:

1) Prevention of wars within the world order and no need for national aremd forces.

2) The unavoidable merging of evonomies and markets, causes free flow of goods (products) and therefore lower prices.

3) The necessity of a unify healthsystem and drug plan as well as phar-maceuticals for all citizents.

4) The urgent necessity for standardisation of labour regulations in all companies in the world order, including working hours, length of vacation, vacation pay, health care, retirement age, ect.

This eliminates the greatest obstacle, peventing us from fully utilizing the capacity of the population, namely interst on debt, which was imposed by the capitalistig Elite and at the same time contributes to bridging the gab between rich and poor. The word "Profit" must be anathema in the "World Government", because it is not capital that is the purpose of yield, but rather welfare of the individuel citizen.

It is unlikely, that switching from today's economic order, with the accumulating of debt amounting to trillions of dollars as a whole, to a "World Government" as desribed above, would go off without serious social and political strife. Those powers in Finance, Banks, Economics and International Corporations, who today rule as they see fit and would like nothing better then to rule the world, will fight with all their intrigue and might. To keep their "Sinecure", thy will not shy away from spreding the most malicious lies and shedding crocodile tears. It is to be hoped, that no "third world war" is necessarily to rekindle the idea of a "World Government" as discussed here.

All those, who are positive understanding and in favor of this proposal for a "World Government" must in words and in deets support the loudable aim within the spirit of "social justice."

It is well known, that the idea of democracy grew in people's mind for centuries, before achieving it's present recognition. In the same way, the idea of "social justice" must be spread to the peoples of the world, by any means of propaganda and influence because, as already mentioned, the will and the desire for a "World Government" must com from the grass rootes, from the masses and not from the upper classes and rulers to day.

After a "World Government" is established, the individual citizen must be educated from the cradle about "social justice;. They must learn compassion and mercy, contribution and cooperation and not the capitalistic rule "the winner taks all". At the same time it can be assumed, that the money system is also changed, according to the rules of "common dividend" (social credit) and the pursuit of the "Dollar" is lessened. Then even the member states und the "World Government" itself, must have laws and regulations for the benefit of all and which must be observed. Since the people in a "World Government", whether smart and energetic or spiritaly not ap to date, are all humen beings afflicted with virtues and vices, which makes also a police force a necessity for each member state and the "World Government" as well. It is not and must not become a playground for eccentric and asociale elemente.

Some points that are undesirable in the social structure of the "World Government" and must be observed and implemented:

1 Possesion of weapons of any kind, with the exception of those employed in public safety, forst rangers and hunters, is undesirable.

2 Lotteries and casinos are undesirable.

3 Public health care for every individual is a matter of course.

4 The media, like radio,television and all publcations must be encouraged to prais "virtues" and condemn "vices".

5   Whether large or small, states in the "World Government" are equal with respect to social justice. Larger states with an accordingly strong and more influential economy, do not have the right to dominate other states.

6   The sociale achievements of today's modern ore advenced nations, like "freedom of speech and religion", to assemble or the freedom to form professional associations such as labour unions etc. are accepted.

7   Private property of any kind is respected in the "World Government".

8   A larger Union of states like the "World Government" is also able to intervene earlier and more successful with help after natural disasters such as earthquackes, tidal waves, hurricanes, volcanic eruptions, droughts, etc.

In order to create the agencies of power in the "World Governmnent", parties must be created whose politican's, after a democratic election, determine the type and direction of policies based on the will of the people.

All the positive forces in the "World Government" are called to exercise the greatest vigilance in order to prevent destructive forces from unfolding and causing harm and unrest in the population, like oratorical agitators, those obsessed with obtaining power and canning elements. The "World Government" must be protected from destruction within.

When God gave Mannkind "Freedem",
then with the obligation of greatest vigilanc,
especely against people whit Power in the states.

Starting whit the age of 20, all citizen of the "World Government" are taking part in a "Point System", executed by the states. For each subsequent year, it awards a point, if no misdemanor's were reported that are not in line with "Social Justice". The greatest number accumulated points permits the individual to enjoy social adventages such as a higher pension payments or other rewards as the case might be.

Good conduct must be rewarded.

Natural, the central government, apart from the states governments of the "World Government", must receive extra ordinary power from the electorate, the people, so that orders from it have teeth and are obeyed to the letter of the law against the culprit. A repeat of the wicked experience with the "League of Nations" after World War I and the wretched show of the "United Nations" after World War II, has to be avoided at all cost.

That is my contribution to the subject and I cherish the hope, that this essay was not written in vain and that utopia will become reality, sooner or later. To abolish the slavery took several centuries until it was achieved, lets hope, it will this time not take that long. In conclusion a poem by LUDWIG UHLAND:

Freedom that I believe in,
that fills my heart.
Com with your light,
sweet angelig vision.
No wich to the troubled world,
merely dance in the heavenly firmament.

www.ingramcontent.com/pod-product-compliance
Lightning Source LLC
Chambersburg PA
CBHW022004170526
45157CB00003B/1139